PASS THE DRIVING TEST

LONDON
IAN ALLAN LTD

GORDON COLE

First published 1984
Second edition published 1990

ISBN 0 7110 1916 9

Published by Ian Allan Ltd, Shepperton, Surrey;
and printed by Ian Allan Printing Ltd at their works at Coombelands in Runnymede, England.

Contents

Preface

This book complements my LP Record/Cassette *The Driving Test and How to Pass it*, which went on general release in July 1978.

There have been many books on learning to drive, but none have explained the marking procedure — how or on what points a person could fail the driving test — in such precise detail. Written by someone who has been a driving examiner and driving instructor for 30 years, this book will take you through the test in explicit detail with the marking in mind; any doubt you might have about any part of the test will be made clear for you. Not only will novice drivers find this book invaluable, but driving instructors, and drivers who feel their driving procedure should be brought up to date, will benefit too.

One person's attitude to driving might be completely different from another's, but to be able to reach a high standard, the novice driver has to develop certain qualities which have to become second nature. These qualities are:

- The responsibility for the safety of other road users and pedestrians.
- To be able to concentrate on driving at all times.
- To anticipate the actions of other road users and pedestrians.
- To have patience and show courtesy and consideration towards other road users and pedestrians.
- To have confidence and ability to handle the vehicle being driven and to be able to cope with any situation that may arise by using the controls of the vehicle with maximum smoothness and efficiency.

If you can develop these qualities, you will have the right attitude for good driving.

The aim of the following chapters is to get the reader's standard of driving to as near perfection as possible, regardless of any point of view which you might have about the test. You must always bear in mind the object and purpose of the test: to prove to the examiner that you can handle a vehicle safely, observe the *Highway Code* and put its contents into practice, show courtesy and consideration for other road users, and that you are competent to drive.

If you can do this on your test, you will pass first time.

Acknowledgements

I thank my friends most sincerely for the time and patience necessary to arrange the photographs. In particular I should like to thank the following: for acting the part of the novice driver and the second vehicle driver — Neil Taylor, Mark Williams, Michael Laporte, Keith Holland; for acting the part of the Driving Test Examiner, John Bromfield; and a special thank you to Vauxhall Motors, Luton, who so kindly supplied the vehicles. All photography was by the author using Leica R4 and R5 cameras. All images were taken on Fuji Professional film processed by Kingsley Michael, Letchworth, Herts. The 'L' roof sign was supplied by Ace Signs of Big G Products, Edmonton, London.

Driving tests are conducted throughout the year and in all types of weather, but not in ice, fog or snow.

Most of all, however, I would like to thank those members of the general public who — unwittingly! — helped make the prearranged traffic situations more realistic for the photographer!

Tests are conducted during the hours of daylight, but the light can vary from bright sunshine to premature darkness. When visibility becomes poor the test is halted by the examiner due to inadequate daylight. Therefore the photography for this book was undertaken at different times of the day and months, using the natural light available at the time, thus giving the reader an insight into the different lighting conditions that can be expected when a driving test is taken.

To do the best for their pupils, driving instructors should ensure that some tuition is given in adverse weather conditions and at night, and on all types of roads.

Gordon Cole

Introduction

A novice driver who is having driving lessons with a professional driving instructor, should be told at the beginning of each lesson the format and objectives of the lesson (lesson plan) for that session. The pupil will then be aware of the content of the lesson. The pupil should be encouraged to ask questions during and at the end of a lesson, and the instructor should ask the pupil questions during and at the end of the lesson. This should be done to confirm that the pupil understands whatever has been covered in the lesson, is made clear. Should any doubt still arise to any part and/or aspect of the lesson, the instructor should clarify the point(s) in question before the pupil leaves the vehicle, otherwise the objective(s) of the lesson will not have been achieved.

The instructor should give praise and/or criticism as and when required.

In 1989 only 51% passed the driving test. What a waste of time and money the 49% who did not pass represents for both examiners and also the candidates who were not up to the required standard!

Some examples why people failed the driving test are:

- The candidate's eyesight did not reach the required standard.
- The vehicle in which the candidate was going to take the test was unsuitable, or its general condition did not comply with the law, or was specially adjusted so that the engine was set to run fast.
- No 'L' plates were displayed, or if they were they were displayed incorrectly or obstructed the candidate's view to the front or rear.
- The seat belts were dirty or twisted so that they could not be adjusted easily, or were unfit to wear, or did not comply with the law, or the vehicle did not have seat belts fitted and thus contravened the law.
- The candidate's driving was not up to the required standard and failed the test on a Control, Road Procedure, Observation or Safety fault.
- Incorrect decisions were made which inconvenienced, were potentially dangerous to, or directly dangerous to other road users or pedestrians.
- Abandoned tests, where the examiner or the candidate terminated the test in the interest of Road Safety.
- The candidate did not know the contents of the *Highway Code*, or other motoring matters put by the examiner.
- While on test, the candidate was involved in an accident which was his or her fault.

There is no substitute for professional tuition and practice from an approved driving instructor. This sort of instruction is easy to get — you will find a list of driving schools in your local telephone directory. Driving instruction from a relative might seem cheaper, but is it in the end? Your driving licence is a lifetime investment and is worth investing in.

This book will help you do that, and assist you in passing your test first time. Remember, good drivers are trained not born! The book *Drive and Survive* by Gordon Cole, published by Kogan Page, a multi-choice question book (200 illustrations) will enable new drivers to gain experience in the safety of their homes.

Car Sympathy

A thorough understanding of the workings of an engine and transmission system is of the utmost importance. This knowledge, combined with intelligent use of the accelerator, clutch, gears and brakes, will enable the novice driver to change gear smoothly and thus gain maximum efficiency from the engine. In turn this will give economical motoring — part of the ultimate aim of good driving.

A driver who is not in unison with their car, who do not understand the basic mechanics and who cannot use the right controls at the right time for any given road situation, will find a dangerous lack of co-ordination between themselves and their vehicles which could easily lead to serious problems.

The driver and vehicle must be in unison at all times.

1 Preparing for the test

Applying for a Driving Test

When you are confident in your driving, and you feel you are competent to take a driving test, you will have to apply for an appointment. There is an official application form for a driving test appointment — form DL26 — which can be obtained from any post office or traffic area office. The form is self-explanatory, but needs to be studied carefully, especially the sections concerning the different types of vehicles within each group, as you might want to drive other vehicles at a later date. If you wish to drive a vehicle not included in the list, you should obtain form D100 for advice. Remember to answer all the questions and enclose the appropriate fee when you send your application — if you do not, the form will be returned to you for completion. The fee for a test appointment is displayed in all driving test centres and traffic area offices.

When completed send the form to the address given and not to the driving test centre, as this will delay your application. If you are deaf or dumb state this under the 'Disabilities' section of the form. You will then receive a DL28 — an appointment card — which is a receipt and confirmation of your driving test appointment. If you do not receive this within 21 days of your application you should make enquiries at the traffic area office to which you sent your application.

It is of the utmost importance that you comply with the time stated on your appointment card. If you arrive late, the test will be cancelled, because there will not be sufficient time to conduct it, and you will forfeit your test fee. Allow yourself time to park your vehicle and, if you do not know the location of the test centre, find out well before the day of your test.

In the event of fog, ice or snow your test appointment could be cancelled and you are advised to telephone the test centre. The telephone number is on your appointment card.

The documents you will need when you arrive at the test centre are: driving licence, appointment card (DL28), insurance certificate and if you have been excluded from the Motor Vehicles (Wearing of Seat Belts) Regulations 1982, a valid medical seat belt exemption certificate from your doctor. Have these documents readily available just in case the examiner asks to see them. If you take your test in a driving school car, the instructor will have the insurance certificate and so there will be no need to ask for it.

The Condition and Suitability of the Vehicle

The vehicle you use for the driving test must be mechanically sound and comply with the law. Here are some of the things that are considered to make a vehicle mechanically unsound or unsuitable for the test:

- No 'L' plates, or incorrectly displayed ones.
- 'L' plates obstructing the driver's view to the front or rear.
- Stop lamps, or direction indicators, not working properly.
- Lens or lenses missing or broken on stop lamps or direction indicators.
- Windscreen wiper blades missing, or not working properly.
- Worn tyres, and other tyre faults that do not meet the requirements of the law.
- Dual accelerator pedal or lever not removed.
- Engine running too fast.
- Improper seating for the examiner.
- A left-hand drive vehicle without a mirror fitted on the offside. The driver of a left-hand drive vehicle must be able to make full and proper use of such a mirror before making any right turn manoeuvre.
- A commercial vehicle which is loaded or partially loaded, or which exceeds 7.5 tonnes permissible maximum weight.
- Seat belts that do not comply with the law, or which are dirty, tangled or not fit to wear.
- The interior and/or exterior mirror(s) missing, therefore not complying with the law. In any case, a vehicle (other than a motorcycle) first used on or after 1 June 1978 must be equipped with an offside external mirror and an internal mirror, firmly affixed.

It is illegal and dangerous to drive a motor vehicle which has a dirty windscreen, but a lot of test candidates arrive at test centres with vehicles which can only be described as filthy, both outside and in. A dirty vehicle is a neglected vehicle; a neglected vehicle is a dangerous vehicle.

One does not give a good impression either if there are lucky charms or mascots hanging from the interior mirror; these can swing about in front of the driver, distracting him and obscuring the view of the road, which is potentially dangerous. This also applies to stickers on windscreen or windows; these often impair vision.

If you are using a driving school car, all these points will be looked after by your instructor. If you do decide to take the test in your own vehicle, pay attention to the details!

Pre-Test Nerves

Understandably, people worry about all sorts of things on the day of their test. If they let these pre-test nerves get the better of them, then they have got a problem.

Pre-test nerves affect people in many different ways: some people are not aware they are suffering from them, but a lot of people do. The signs and symptoms of test nerves are:

- Eyesight can become impaired.
- Dry mouth.
- Perspiration in palms of hands.
- Increased heart beat.
- Inability to concentrate.
- More frequent use of the toilet.
- A pale or very red complexion.
- Shaking and loss of control of faculties.
- Frequent blinking.
- People get very emotional.
- Speech is affected.

In extreme cases some drivers are unable to react to a sudden situation at all; this is known as freezing.

These are the signs of worry or nerves and will affect your driving. As mentioned previously, if you are confident and competent in your driving you have nothing to worry about. Never take drugs or alcohol to counteract worry or nerves; to do so could be very dangerous, and is illegal.

If you have a physical disability, you may find the circumstances of a driving test rather trying; the examiner will understand your difficulties and will be as helpful and considerate as he can.

If you do not understand or speak English very well, or if you are deaf and dumb, you may take an interpreter with you, but he will only be there to help you and the examiner understand each other, he cannot take any part in the test itself; if he does the test will be terminated.

Right:
At this test centre there are parking facilities for driving test candidates.

Introduction to the Driving Test and the Driving Examiner

A word here about the driving examiner — he will be sympathetic and understanding, but will confine himself to the business in hand, which will entail directing you over an approved test route, asking you to manoeuvre your vehicle at particular places. At the end of the test, he will ask you questions on the *Highway Code* and other motoring matters, and then ask you to identify some traffic signs from pictures.

The driving test takes approximately 35 minutes overall.

There is an extensive system of supervision for the test which takes several forms. Occasionally a supervising examiner will sit in with your examiner during the test. If this happens do not worry, he will not take any part in the test, but is there to see that your examiner does his job precisely as the Department wishes it to be done. Listen carefully to what the examiner asks you to do, and carry out the instruction as well as you can, and your test will be as fair as it can be made. The supervising examiner will ask your permission if he can accompany you on your test; you can decline but very few people do. The examiner will not give you any encouragement or criticism, he is there to observe and report your driving ability which will be done impartially.

On the day of your test, arrive at the waiting room in good time, so that you give yourself time to relax. A natural point here is that not all driving test centres have a toilet for public use, therefore you may have to walk some distance to the nearest toilet. Allow time for this, otherwise you could find yourself in an embarrassing situation, and then be late for your test.

People naturally worry about all sorts of things before and during their tests — whether they are doing things correctly or worrying about something unforeseen happening. While you are thinking on these lines your concentration is impaired and you will miss very important situations before they occur. Experience helps you get over this and if you have had plenty of good instruction, and you and your driving instructor feel confident about your driving, you will be able to concentrate on the job in hand. Put baldly, provided you do not inconvenience, or make any potentially dangerous or dangerous faults either on safety, control or road procedure, to any other road user or pedestrian during your test, and you answer the questions on the *Highway Code* and other motoring matters which the examiner will put to you, and explain the meaning of the traffic signs which the examiner will show pictures of, then you will pass your test first time. *Drive and Survive* by Gordon Cole is a multi-choice question book which enables new drivers to gain experience in their homes.

In and from the Waiting Room

At the time stated on your appointment card, the examiner will meet you in the waiting room. You will be asked to sign your name on his attendance register and he will lend you his pen to do this. Your signature is confirmation that you have attended and started your driving test. The examiner will then ask you to lead the way to your vehicle. On the way you will be asked if you have any physical disability that is not declared on your application form. This is to confirm that you have suffered no physical disability which could affect your ability to drive since completing your application form.

Comply with the requirements of the eyesight test

As you get near to where your vehicle is parked, the examiner will ask you which vehicle is yours, to make sure he does not ask you to read your own numberplate. A point of warning here; if you put on a pair of glasses to read this numberplate then you must keep them on throughout the test. It is not permitted to wear glasses just to read the numberplate. You will be asked to read a numberplate well over the prescribed distance required

Below:
At this test centre there are no parking facilities. Allow yourself extra time to park your vehicle, as in some areas this can be difficult.

by law. If you cannot read it then the examiner will take you a little nearer, and will ask you to read the same numberplate again. If you still cannot read it, then the examiner will have to return to his office to get the official tape measure to measure the exact distance from the numberplate to the point where you should be able to read it, ie 67ft (20.42m) for letters and figures 3⅛in (79mm) high on the numberplate or 75ft (22.86m) for letters and figures 3½in (88mm) high on the numberplate. If you cannot read the numberplate at the prescribed distance, then you immediately fail the test because your eyesight does not reach the required standard. Indeed, you will have been committing an offence even driving to the test centre. For not being able to comply with the regulations regarding eyesight for drivers, your test will be terminated, and you will lose your test fee. Candidates who are dumb or who cannot read and write will be requested to draw the letters and numbers with pen and paper supplied by the examiner.

If you can read the numberplate, then the examiner will ask you to get into your vehicle.

Summary

Learn as much as possible about the basic mechanics and controls of a motor vehicle, then you will appreciate why and what you are doing when you use the controls.

Complete the test application form and send the appropriate fee — not in cash, but by cheque or money order.

Plan your lessons so that you will be up to the required standard before the day of your test. Your driving instructor will advise you when you should apply for a test appointment.

If the test appointment date offered is not suitable you should return the appointment card straight away to the address shown. You must give 10 whole working days' notice, excluding the day the traffic area office receives your cancellation, otherwise you will forfeit your test fee.

Make sure your vehicle is suitable for the test and that it is clean.

Test nerves — your mental and physical state at the time of testing must be borne in mind. It is of the utmost importance that you should relax and not worry about the test, otherwise it will have mental effects — you will not be able to concentrate properly — and physical ones which could affect the way you operate the controls of the vehicle, resulting in jerky movements and impaired control.

Arrive at the test centre in good time and remember that not all test centres have toilet or parking facilities.

Check your eyesight well before the day of your test.

Do not try to hold a conversation with the examiner while you are driving, as this could be distracting for you and affect your concentration and driving.

It is illegal to drive a motor vehicle while under the influence of alcohol and drugs. Do not smoke while you are driving.

Anyone who offers a bribe to a driving examiner to procure a pass will be prosecuted.

Right:
When you have read the numberplate correctly, you will be asked to get into your vehicle.

2 Moving off Safely and the Emergency Stop

The Cockpit Drill

Take proper precautions before starting the engine

As you approach your vehicle, the examiner will complete some paperwork before he gets in. While he is doing that get into the vehicle.

Once the examiner has got in he will give you the first instruction, 'Follow the road ahead unless traffic signs direct you otherwise, or unless I ask you to turn, which I will do in good time. Move off when you're ready, please'. Now is the time to carry out your cockpit drill so the examiner can see that you take proper precautions before starting the engine. The cockpit drill is:

(1) Doors properly closed (the examiner will make sure his door is closed, there is no need to lean across him to check); make sure your door is closed.
(2) Seat properly adjusted, so you can operate all the pedals and other controls safely and conveniently.
(3) Adjust the interior mirror to get maximum rear view observation, without having to make excessive movements with your body or head. The examiner will have the experience to know if you are looking in the mirror or not. You do not have to move your head like a boxer!
(4) Check to make sure the handbrake is on (applied).
(5) Check to make sure the gear lever is in neutral.
(6) Put your seat belt on, unless of course you are exempt from wearing one and hold a valid medical exemption certificate from a doctor.

It is permissible to remove the seat belt when you are about to manoeuvre the vehicle — this particularly applies to the reversing exercise — but once the exercise has been completed you must wear the seat belt again, otherwise you will be breaking the law.

Left:
To check your seat position, push your clutch pedal to the floor. You should be able to do this without having to stretch your leg or feel uncomfortable. You should be able to reach all other controls from the correct seating position.

Below:
The best way to adjust the mirror is by using the index finger and thumb of the left hand. Do not put your fingers on the mirror as you adjust it. Without moving your head, adjust the mirror for the best view to the rear, especially to the offside.

If you do remove your seat belt to manoeuvre your vehicle, the most logical way to put it back on again after completing the exercise is to pull up parallel with the kerb, apply the handbrake, move the gear lever into the neutral position and stop the engine. When you have put the seat belt on, restart the engine and carry out the examiner's instructions, making sure it is safe to move off.

When you have completed the cockpit drill, you will then know it is safe to start the engine and get ready to move off. If safe to do so, proceed on the directions of the examiner.

Before going on any further, let us go through two more items of importance — the Driving Test Report Form, and what is meant by 'Make Proper use of the Controls' which you will need to know to move away safely and under control.

The Driving Test Report Form

The examiner will have a Driving Test Report Form — form DL25 — on his lap, which will have your name on it, plus other relevant information relating to your test. There are many myths about the driving test report sheet and what the examiner writes on it. In fact the marking procedure is quite simple: the report sheet is marked in three different ways, each particular mark represents the seriousness of fault made. Clearly we cannot divulge exactly what the marks mean — and anyway you should not try to see what the examiner is writing during your test — but broadly there are three different types of faults a candidate can make at any one time during the test, and the seriousness of the fault committed will determine what category mark is made on the report form. All the examiner is doing is making note of any fault(s) made by the candidate and it should be appreciated that the examiner does not actually fail anyone: the candidates fail themselves. The three different categories of fault which a driver can make are:

Minor Fault

A minor fault is a mistake which does not involve any other road user or pedestrian or cause any inconvenience or danger.

For example, a candidate moves away from the kerb without looking round to check the blind spot and therefore acted without knowing it was safe to move away. In this particular situation no other road user or pedestrian was involved.

Serious Fault (a failure mark)

A serious fault occurs when the candidate has caused or is going to cause a *potentially* dangerous situation or inconvenience to another road user or pedestrian.

For example, a candidate emerges at a junction without taking effective observation, and could have caused another road user or pedestrian to take evasive action. In other words a dangerous situation *has not* occurred, but could well have done so.

Dangerous Fault (a failure mark)
A dangerous fault is made when a candidate *has* created a dangerous situation to any other road user or pedestrian.

For example, a candidate is about to turn right, underestimates the speed of an oncoming vehicle and turns across its path, therefore forcing the other road user to brake hard or change course to avoid a collision.

Being unable to comply with the requirements of the eyesight test, with or without the aid of glasses or contact lenses, is also deemed a serious fault, as is being unable to give the correct answers to the oral test of knowledge of the *Highway Code* and other motoring matters. It is extremely important that you know the contents of the *Highway Code*, so that you can put its advice into practice while driving.

Occasionally a mistake can be double-marked. In other words a test candidate makes a serious fault — for example, by not positioning the vehicle correctly during normal driving. This involves two faults on the DL24 form for (1) steering, and (2) positioning the vehicle correctly during normal driving.

The Controls

Make proper use of accelerator/clutch/gears/ footbrake/steering

Accelerator
The accelerator should be used with reasonable smoothness. Do not press the pedal suddenly, especially when moving off. When accelerating, do so smoothly and progressively as the situation demands and do not accelerate while another vehicle is overtaking you. It is also important that you should be able to ease off the accelerator smoothly when slowing down. Never use too much accelerator at the wrong time or place, as misuse of the accelerator is a fault that could be potentially dangerous. A test candidate who has the expertise to use the accelerator and other controls individually or in conjunction with other controls correctly and at the right time and place, will have the vehicle under control at all times.

If you take your test in a vehicle fitted with automatic transmission, you might have to use the 'kick-down' procedure if you want to overtake or pass another vehicle quickly. A jerk is sometimes experienced while using the kick-down procedure and this will be taken into consideration. It will not be classed as a fault, unless there is obvious misuse of the accelerator.

Clutch
The clutch must be used smoothly and correctly, especially when moving off, changing gear — in conjunction with the accelerator — and stopping — in conjunction with the brake pedal. You should be able to control the clutch correctly and operate it with reasonable smoothness. Do not suddenly release the pedal, rest your foot on it while driving, or coast with the clutch down. You must release it after changing gear, particularly on the approach to junctions. Misuse of the clutch could be potentially dangerous.

Gears
The gears must be used in accordance with the engine speed and road speed at which the vehicle is travelling. You should be in the correct gear at the right time and place in accordance with the prevailing traffic and state of the road. You should plan your driving well ahead, so you will be aware of and be able to anticipate the actions of other road users and pedestrians, thus giving you time to change gear if and when the situation demands. Do not look down at the controls when changing gear. In a built-up area there is no need to use the 5th gear while on test if you have a five-speed gearbox. Improper use of the gears could be potentially dangerous.

Do not make late or hurried use of the gears on the approach to a junction or hazard, or change gear too early. After changing gear do not coast with the clutch down, you should plan your driving so that you give yourself time and distance to be able to release the clutch pedal, so that the gear you have selected can engage properly. This implies particularly on the approach to junctions: see page 68.

Do not select a gear which would be unsuitable for the conditions prevailing, ie approaching a sharp bend in a high gear, when a lower gear would be more suitable and would give you more control of the vehicle. Do not race or labour the engine when a higher or lower gear should be used. Do not change gear while going round a corner unless you have stopped to give way to a pedestrian or other traffic.

Speed should be reduced by proper use of the footbrake. It is potentially dangerous to change down through the gears whilst braking on the approach to a hazard, speed should be reduced then a gate change made. That is, 4th to 2nd, 3rd to 1st gear. Whatever gear is selected it should match that of the road speed of the vehicle.

Far left:
The ideal sitting position — the driver's hands are at a ten to two position (as on a clock face), arms slightly bent. The left leg should be comfortable when the clutch pedal is pressed fully down. The leg should not be straight but slightly bent and the driver's back should be well supported by the seat. When you turn the steering wheel you must pass the wheel from one hand to the other. This is called the push and pull method. You must never lazily cross your hands while turning the wheel as you could lose control of the steering. Make sure you are wearing your seat belt if you are required by law to do so.

If you take your test in a vehicle which has automatic transmission, you should be able to move the gear selector and select the appropriate gear without looking down at the gear lever — this also applies to a vehicle fitted with a manual gearbox. Use the gears to suit the prevailing conditions. Slow the road speed of the vehicle down by proper use of the footbrake and then change into a lower gear; it is bad driving to change gear while in the initial stage of braking.

Footbrake

The footbrake must be used smoothly and progressively and in good time. Do not brake late or make hurried and harsh use of the footbrake. Never brake so late that you endanger the hazard you should be stopping for, or endanger the traffic behind you because of your sudden late braking. On a vehicle which has automatic transmission you must brake in good time so that you give the lower gears time to engage; this applies particularly when approaching junctions. Plan your driving so you can brake smoothly and in good time. The use of the heel and toe (heel on the brake and toe on the accelerator) when braking and changing gear is not good driving and can be dangerous.

Above:
This learner is driving the correct distance from the kerb. Do not drive so close that the wheels are in the gutter. This can be potentially dangerous.

Right:
Do not rest your arm on the door while driving, or steer with one hand when there is no need or reason to do so.

Far right:
Do not cross your hands when turning the steering wheel. For safety reasons it is best to use the push-pull method to turn the wheel.

If you drive a vehicle fitted with automatic transmission you are advised to use your right foot to operate the accelerator and brake pedal and keep your left foot away from the pedals. The only exception to this rule is when you are manoeuvring the vehicle very slowly; then you may need to use your left foot on the brake pedal to help you keep control of the vehicle while your right foot is operating the accelerator pedal.

Handbrake
The handbrake should be applied with the pawl release operated (button pushed in), which will prevent wear to the ratchet. You should be able to release the handbrake in conjunction with the accelerator and clutch so that you move off smoothly without rolling back when on a gradient, or stalling the engine. Always apply the handbrake when the vehicle is stationary, to prevent it rolling forward or backward unexpectedly; do not forget to release the handbrake at the right time.

Vehicles fitted with automatic transmission are known to 'creep' when stationary, with the engine ticking over and the gear selector lever in D, L or R (or an equivalent position). To prevent the vehicle moving unexpectedly, the handbrake should be applied and the gear selector lever moved into neutral position.

Steering and Steering Faults
You should steer a steady course: do not wander from one lane to another or straddle another lane. When turning a corner, turn the steering wheel using the push and pull method, do not let the steering wheel turn back on its own accord or turn the steering wheel in short jerky movements — and do not cross your hands while turning the wheel. Never turn the steering wheel while the vehicle is stationary — this is lazy and puts a lot of excess strain on the steering linkage.

While the engine is running you should never take both hands off the steering wheel at the same time for any reason — whether the vehicle is stationary or moving. Keep both hands on the wheel at all times, except when changing gear, giving a hand signal or using any other control.

When practically possible — ie unless it is impossible because of a bus lane or lane markings or hazard — steer a course so that your nearside wheels are about one metre from the kerb.

When driving along you can — after making effective use of the mirror — look over your left and right shoulder before changing direction. This is to confirm that it is safe to change direction. You must steer a steady course while making this observation; if your vehicle changes course while you are looking over your shoulder, you could create a potentially dangerous situation.

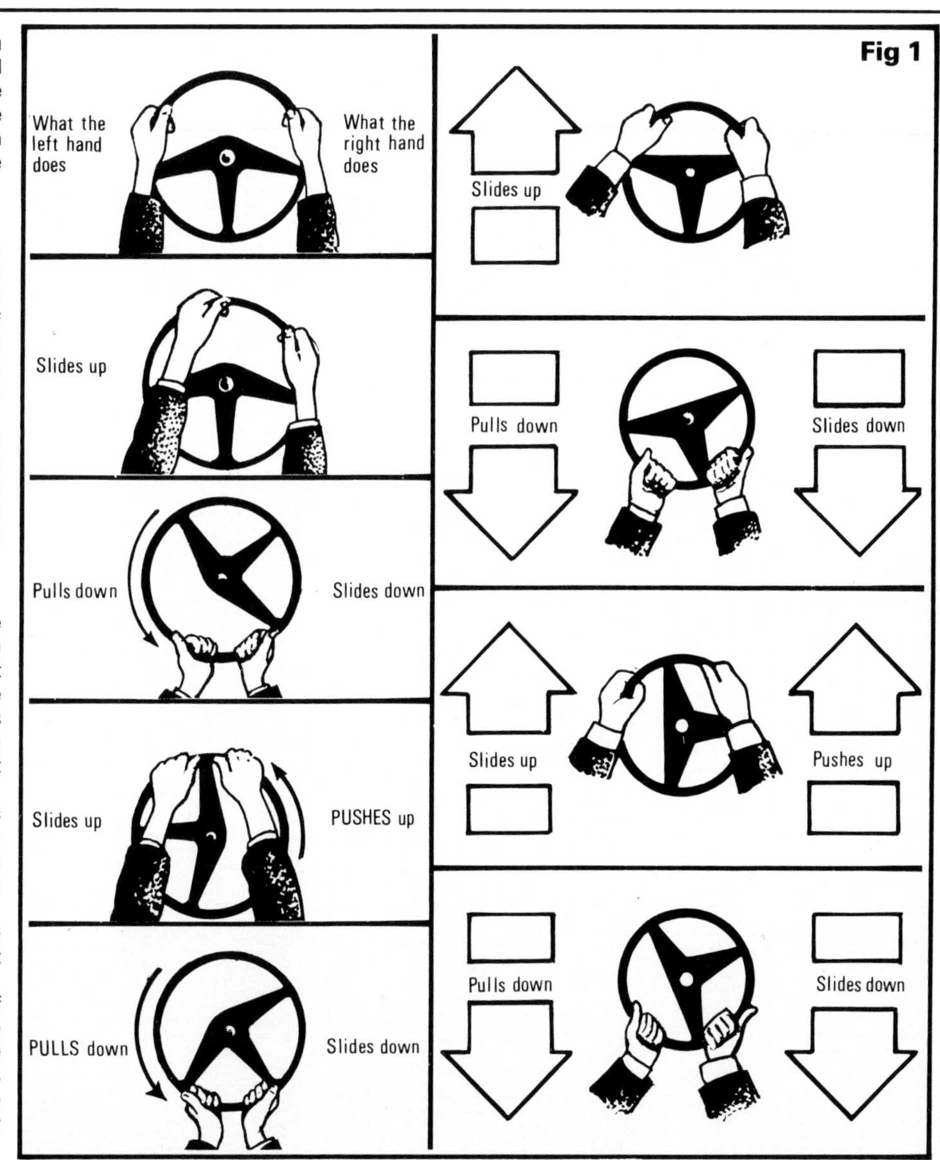

The push and pull method of steering.

Turning Left Faults

Above:
This driver started to turn the steering wheel too early or has turned it too much. This is known as oversteering.

Below:
This driver started to turn the steering wheel too late or has not turned it enough. This is called understeering.

Turning Left Faults

Turning Right Faults

Turning Right Faults

Above right:
This driver has started to turn right too late, and has gone past the road he wanted to enter. This steering fault is called a 'Swan's Neck'. This particular example has caused another road user inconvenience and could therefore be potentially dangerous.

Below right:
This driver has positioned his vehicle incorrectly for turning right, therefore creating potential danger.

General Steering Faults

Far left:
Steer a steady course round bends. Do not cut across a bend like this driver, who has created a potentially dangerous situation to oncoming traffic.

Left:
After completing any left or right turn, your position in the road should be well to the left if it is safe to do so – unlike this learner who has not made proper use of the steering, and has therefore forced another driver to take evasive action.

Left:
When overtaking another vehicle, wait until you can see the vehicle you have passed in your interior mirror, then you will know it is safe to return to the left. Do not cut in like this driver. If you cannot overtake safely, don't. Wait until the road ahead of you is clear and safe.

Above:
When passing a stationary vehicle, allow a safe distance between your vehicle and the stationary one when possible. Allow for other drivers' mistakes. Not allowing adequate clearance to stationary vehicles is a control fault and therefore a double marking fault.

Above right:
A common steering fault is drifting in to the middle of the road and then back to the left again. Steer a steady course when practically possible. Do not drift.

Left:
When you have a clear road ahead of you, do not weave in and out between parked vehicles because you will get boxed in by passing traffic — as this learner has been. Always steer a straight course when the situation allows you to.

Far left, top
This learner is driving too close to the kerb and has created danger to a pedestrian who could have crossed the road without first looking. This is also a 'position the vehicle correctly during normal driving' fault.

Far left, bottom:
The movements of pedestrians are very unpredictable, so make allowances for them. This driver has not and is driving too near to the left for the conditions prevailing. Note the pedestrian who has walked out between the parked cars.

Above
Some test routes have a width restriction to stop heavy goods vehicles using the road. It is important that you steer a steady course as you go through the restriction and you know the width of the vehicle you are driving.

Left:
On some open roads you may see this sign. If you do, be extra careful as you pass cyclists who could be suddenly blown about. A strong side wind will affect your steering.

Above:
Steer a steady course round corners. Do not swing out before or after a corner. This driver has swung out, thereby creating a dangerous situation.

Right:
This driver is steering a steady course with safety while turning left.

Moving Off Safely

Move away safely/under control

Once you have completed your cockpit drill, start your engine and make sure it is running at normal tick-over speed before selecting first gear. If the engine is ticking over properly, push the clutch pedal down to the floor, select first gear and put your hand back on the steering wheel. Press the accelerator pedal down slightly and hold it steady. The engine now should be running at a faster rate, the exact amount of power determined by the road conditions — whether you intend to move off uphill, downhill or from level ground. Now let the clutch pedal come up slowly until you hear the tone of the engine deepen. This is called the 'biting point'. Hold your foot still. The ball of your foot should be in the middle of the pedal and your heel on the floor if you can, as this will give you greater control of the clutch pedal movement. You are now ready to move off, and now is the time to make sure it is safe to do so, by looking in your interior mirror to see what traffic is behind you. If there is traffic visible in your mirror wait until it has gone and when you cannot see any more traffic in your mirror, look over your right and left shoulders at the blind spots to check again before moving off. The blind spots are areas behind you that the mirror does not show. While this observation is being carried out, it is very important that the car does not move and that your feet are steady on the pedals.

If all is clear, check the road ahead. If all is still clear, release the handbrake, put your hand back on the steering wheel and release the clutch pedal slowly. When the clutch pedal has been completely released, use more gradual pressure on the accelerator pedal. That is, of course, if you want the car to go faster. If you start your test in a car park, or with a car park which has an exit with poor visibility, you are advised to move off as slowly and safely as possible, because a vehicle or pedestrian may suddenly cross your path without warning.

The use of signals when moving off is most important. These signals let other road users or pedestrians know what your intentions are. But signals are only warnings and do not give you the right of way. Only use a signal if you think it will help other road users understand your intentions. Do not move off if you will inconvenience or endanger any other road user or pedestrian. If the road is clear of any other road user or pedestrian, no signal is needed to move off.

To sum up, from whatever position, whether you start your driving test in a car park or on the road, you must move off safely and under control. This means making effective use of the mirror and look all round to check any blind spots, checking the road ahead, and then only if you are completely sure it is safe, can you move off safely without causing any inconvenience or danger to any other road user or pedestrian.

Under control means making proper use of the right gear and complete co-ordination of the accelerator, clutch and handbrake so that you move off smoothly and do not roll back on a hill or move off in jerky movements or suddenly take off. If necessary you must use signals (direction indicators) when moving off.

Far left:
It is of the utmost importance that you look in the mirror, and then look round over your right shoulder before moving off, regardless if you have exterior mirrors fitted to your vehicle or not. There is no way that a properly adjusted interior mirror should show you the vehicle emerging from a driveway. This is a good example of why you must look round before moving off.

Above
When you are ready to move away you must do so safely and under control. This means making proper use of the mirror, checking the blind spot so that you do not cause any inconvenience or potential danger to any other road user like this driver. When the road is clear, move off using the controls smoothly.

Left:
If you do not look round before moving off you could create a potentially dangerous situation. Check the blind spot first, before moving off. If in any doubt WAIT.

Observation

Top left:
Use the interior mirror often to see what is behind you.

Below:
Check the blind spot to see if the road behind you is clear of approaching traffic; only when it is safe to do so should you move off.

Top right:
Even if you have exterior mirrors fitted to your vehicle, you must look round before moving off. You should look in the mirror and look round before opening your door to make sure it is safe to do so.

Observation

Top right:
If you start your driving test from a car park, all-round observation must be taken before you move off and as you drive out of it.

Right:
When it is raining, globules of water on the mirror will distort or reduce what can be seen behind you.

Far right:
A rear window that is misted on the inside and running with rainwater on the outside is not an ideal combination for good rear observation. It is the driver's responsibility to take the necessary action to improve his view to the rear.

ELMES
ELMES
E441 CJN
ASTRA
Merit
F858 HBH
VAUXHALL
C615 FBM

Move Off at an Angle

During your test the examiner will ask you to pull up on the left just before a parked vehicle — on the level or on a gradient. It is of the utmost importance that you allow adequate room to be able to move off again without having to manoeuvre your vehicle. This exercise is called 'Move Off at an Angle' which is part of Move Away Safely/Under Control and is one of the official manoeuvres you are required to do as part of the test.

The Natural Drive

Once you have moved off, the next instruction the examiner will give you will be to turn left or right. The procedure for approaching junctions is explained later under the heading 'Act Properly at Road Junctions'.

The first part of the driving test is called the 'Natural Drive' and lasts about one mile. Each test centre has a number of different routes which can be used at any given time and one could be longer than another. However, regardless of length all routes are equal to each other in content.

After you have been driving for about one mile the examiner will ask you to ***'pull up on the left at a convenient place, please'*** or ***'pull up along here, just before the lamp-post/telegraph pole/etc please'***.

The reason for this stop is that you will be doing your first exercise very shortly — the 'Emergency Stop'. Carry out your procedure for stopping and pull up on the left near to the kerb. Apply the handbrake and move the gear lever (selector) into neutral and put both hands back on the steering wheel.

Above:

Before moving off you must make effective use of the mirror and look round to check the blind spot and act accordingly on what you see — unlike this 'L' driver who has moved off into the path of another vehicle.

Right:

If there is any other road user or pedestrian in front of you, let them pass before you move off. This driver did not notice the car coming towards him, moved off and created a potentially dangerous situation.

The Emergency Stop

Stop the vehicle in an emergency/promptly/ under control/making proper use of foot brake

The examiner will give you the instructions for this exercise, ie ***'Very shortly I shall ask you to stop as in an emergency; the signal will be like this*** (the examiner will touch the dashboard or windscreen with a small book or board) and at the same time say STOP. ***When I do that, stop immediately under full control as though a child had run off the pavement.*** Move off when you are ready, please'.

Once asked, go through the usual moving-off procedures remembering to check in your mirror, and the blind spot by looking over your right shoulder. If all is clear, recheck your mirror, release the handbrake, put your hand back on the steering wheel and move off safely and smoothly.

As you build your speed up to about 20mph (30km/h), the examiner will look over his right shoulder to check there is no traffic following close behind you. If the road is clear the examiner will say 'stop' and touch the dashboard as described earlier. As soon as you hear 'stop' your right foot should come off the accelerator and on to the footbrake as quickly as possible, applying firm and progressive pressure on the pedal. Once you have applied the footbrake, push the clutch pedal to the floor and keep both feet still. As soon as the vehicle has stopped, apply the handbrake, and move the gear lever into neutral, replace your hand on the steering wheel and then take both feet off the pedals. Do not switch the engine off.

Should an emergency arise naturally during the Natural Drive phase of the test, the examiner will decide whether there is any need for a special exercise to be carried out.

You do not have to give any signal or look in your mirror for this exercise as the examiner will have checked the road behind you before he gives you the signal to stop. The Emergency Stop is a *reaction test* and not a *brake test*.

When you have completed the emergency stop exercise the examiner will say, ***'Thank you, I shan't ask you to carry out that exercise again. Drive on when you are ready, please.'*** Remember the moving-off procedure, and if all is clear and safe move off smoothly. The deciding factors which will determine how quickly your vehicle will stop are:

- the condition of the road surface — whether is it coarse or smooth, loose gravel or wet or dry road
- the efficiency of the brakes and the type of brakes fitted to the vehicle
- the condition and type of tyres fitted to the vehicle
- your own reaction time
- uphill of downhill gradient.

Whatever the deciding factors are, you must not brake too hard and lock the wheels causing skidding and possible loss of control of the vehicle. If there is any feeling of the road wheels locking (skidding) come off the brake pedal and reapply the brake, but with less pressure, otherwise you could create a potentially dangerous situation. This is the only exercise throughout the test for which you do not have to check in the mirror before stopping and the word 'stop' is used. If you do the Emergency Stop on a road which carries a lot of traffic, rubber dust and spilt diesel fuel and oil can make the road surface very slippery, and induce skidding. This applies even when the road surface is dry, even more so when the surface is wet. Treat a partially wet road as a wet one, if you are stopping in an emergency.

Above left:
The driver of this vehicle is braking hard. Note how the front of the car dips. At this point the rear wheels could lock and skid. If not corrected, this could lead to loss of control of the vehicle, a potentially dangerous or dangerous fault depending on the circumstances.

Left:
The use of the footbrake should be one positive progressive action and not a succession of rhythmic pumps. This driver has braked too hard, skidded and lost control of his vehicle. Because of the potential danger due to loss of control, it will be marked as a control fault. If the vehicle is fitted with an Anti-Lock Braking System, it prevents the car's wheels from locking and skidding.

Road Surfaces

Top left:
There are many types of road surfaces you could drive on and must be taken into consideration. Be extra careful when braking on a road surface covered in wet leaves which are very slippery. Allow extra stopping distance on this type of road surface, otherwise a potentially dangerous situation will occur.

Bottom left:
Another potential danger — a road surface which has diesel fuel on it; allow extra stopping distance otherwise you will create danger to other road users.

Top right:
If you do the emergency stop on an uphill gradient your stopping distance should obviously be shorter than that on a downhill gradient, subject to the vehicle being in good working order.

Far right:
Your stopping distance will increase if you make an emergency stop on a downhill gradient, even with a vehicle in good working order. Be extra careful when the road surface is wet.

Summary

If you should stall the engine at any time, apply the handbrake and move the gear lever into neutral before restarting the engine.

Do not worry about what the examiner is writing on the report sheet.

Do not accelerate while you are being overtaken.

Never select a higher gear on the approach to a hazard. Always change down into a lower gear before reaching a hazard. Keep both hands on the steering wheel in the initial stages of braking.

Do not grip the steering wheel.

Do not change gear and give an arm signal at the same time.

Move off only when you are sure it is safe to do so. If in doubt, wait.

While doing the emergency stop do not move the gear lever into neutral or apply the handbrake while the vehicle is moving, and do not put the clutch pedal down before applying the footbrake.

When you have to slow your vehicle down, do not put the clutch pedal down and then brake or put the clutch pedal down too early on the approach to a hazard.

Do not turn the steering wheel while your vehicle is stationary.

Do not rest your foot on the clutch pedal while driving. Take your foot away from the pedal when you have used it.

Braking

THINKING DISTANCE at 30 M.P.H.

Distance travelled during reaction time

Time(sec.)	Distance (ft.)	Time(sec.)	Distance (ft.)
·175	7·7	·475	20·9
·2	8·8	·5	22
·225	9·9	·525	23·1
·25	11	·55	24·2
·275	12·1	·575	25·3
·3	13·2	·6	26·4
·325	14·3	·625	27·5
·35	15·4	·65	28·6
·375	16·5	·675	29·7
·4	17·6	·7	30·8
·425	18·7	·725	31·9
·45	19·8	·75	33

REMEMBER—This does not include braking distance which at 30m.p.h is a further 45ft.

TOTAL STOPPING DISTANCE

Distance travelled assuming an about average reaction time

M.P.H	Reaction Distance	Braking Distance	Total Stopping Distance
	ft.	ft.	ft.
20	20	20	40
30	30	45	75
40	40	80	120
50	50	125	175
60	60	180	240
70	70	245	315

REMEMBER—These braking distances only apply on dry road surfaces. On wet roads, they could double.

Thinking Distance

Top:
The action of braking has two components — the thinking distance and the braking distance. The thinking distance can also be called the reacting distance. The moment your eyes recognise danger the information is transmitted to the brain which informs the driver to apply the brake. A typical example is when a driver fails to check if it is safe to reverse, like the one in the photograph. If the driver is alert, immediate action will be taken, otherwise an accident may occur.

Far left:
The average driver will take 0.7sec to respond to a sudden situation. In that time the distance travelled would be 30.8ft for a vehicle travelling at 30mph.

Left:
From the moment the driver applies the brake to the time the vehicle comes to rest is called the stopping distance.

3 Reversing and the Turn in the Road

Reversing

Reverse into a limited opening either to the right or left under control/with due regard to other road users

After the emergency stop you will start the main body of the test which will consist of varying road and traffic conditions. You will have to negotiate different types of junctions which could include roundabouts. It is during this part of the test that you will have to do the next special exercise — the turn in the road, or reverse into a limited opening either to the right or left. Whichever exercise you are asked to do next will depend on the route you are on. Let us examine first the reverse into a limited opening to the left which is presented in diagrammatic form in Fig 2.

Below:
This is the view of the corner from the point where the examiner has asked you to pull up. The nearside wheels should be within 6in of the kerb.

Reverse into a limited opening to the left

As you drive along the examiner will ask you to pull up just before the next road on the left — Position 1 in the diagram. Carry out the stopping procedure. You should pull up at a safe parking distance from the kerb in such a position that you can see into the road on the left. The purpose of this is so that the examiner can see into the road to make sure it is safe and clear for him to give you the next instruction which is, ***'This road on the left is the one into which I should like you to reverse. Drive past it and stop, then back in and continue to drive in reverse gear for some distance, keeping reasonably close to the kerb. Move off when you're ready, please'.*** The examiner will not say anything else until you have reversed into the side road on the left, when he will thank you and ask you to pull up.

To complete this exercise safely you must maintain control of your vehicle and carry out the manoeuvres effectively, with due regard for other road users. If you carry out the following procedures, you will be able to do this simply. Look at the drawing on page 29.

Once the examiner has explained what he would like you to do, move off safely and as you reach Position 2 — ie when you can see the corner you are going to reverse round in your interior mirror, and have positioned your vehicle about 18in away from the kerb, look in the mirror and, if necessary, signal your intentions to stop by using the left turn indicator, pull up and apply the handbrake and move the gear lever into neutral. Do not switch the engine off. Put your hand back on the steering wheel — and look over your left shoulder. Take note where the kerb passes through the bottom of the rear window. When you reverse towards the corner try to keep the kerb in the same position in the window, then you should be able to reverse with reasonable accuracy.

When you look over your left shoulder, you might find this position a bit of a strain on your neck. If it is, then turn the bottom of your body to the left slightly and you will find this more comfortable. The important thing is to be comfortable. It is

A Rounded Corner

Top:
There are three types of corner — rounded, semi-sharp and sharp. You will only be asked to reverse round one of these, but you should be able to cope with any of them.

Far left:
A semi-sharp corner.

Left:
A sharp corner.

permissible, if need be, to rest your left arm on the back of your seat so that you can help keep yourself steady while reversing, but both hands must be used to steer throughout this exercise, unless of course you have a physical disability. However, you must keep your vehicle under control at all times and perform the manoeuvre with due regard to other road users.

Once you have got ready to reverse, and it is safe to do so, move off towards the road in question. As you reach Position 3, check to make sure it is safe to continue reversing. When you are sure the road you are about to reverse into and the road directly behind you are clear, then check your front, in case a vehicle is coming towards you. The reason for this is because the front of your vehicle will swing out as you reverse round the corner.

When you have checked to make sure you will not cause any inconvenience or danger to other road users or pedestrians, continue reversing and follow the kerb round the corner, keeping the rounded kerb passing through the same part of the rear window as shown in the drawing of Position 3. Continue reversing round the corner. Your speed should be that of a slow walking man (under control and with due regard for other road users), the amount of power you will need from your engine will be determined by the camber of the road, whether you are reversing downhill or uphill or on the level. Regardless of the type of camber involved, do not coast with the clutch disengaged or with the gear lever in neutral. Keep reversing round the corner through Position 4, straighten up and continue reversing until you are some way down the road.

When the examiner requests you to pull up, do so still looking out of the rear window. You should not look to the front while reversing. Subject to the road being clear behind you, it is possible that you will have reversed about three to four car lengths from the corner. When you have pulled up, apply the handbrake and move the gear lever into neutral position. Put your hand back on the steering wheel. That is the end of the reversing exercise.

The next instruction the examiner will give you is to continue driving, turning either left or right at the road ahead, depending on the route you are following. Once more, prepare yourself for moving off: check the interior mirror for approaching traffic, look over your right shoulder (blind spot), check the road ahead, and if it is safe to move away, release the handbrake and move off smoothly under control.

After you have started to move off, check your mirror and use the direction indicator to signal your intention to turn left/right, then carry out the rest of the system for approaching a junction (covered in a later chapter). You will now be on route to your next exercise which is the turn round in the road.

Right:
Position One When the examiner completes the instruction for this exercise he will say 'move off when you are ready, please'. He will not say anything else until you reach Position Five where he will ask you to pull up, unless, of course, there is a stationary vehicle. In that case *you* will decide to pull up at a safe distance from the stationary vehicle.

Far right:
Position Two As you pass the corner you are going to reverse round, look in the interior mirror to see if there is any traffic behind you. When you can see the corner in the mirror you will then be the correct distance away from it to pull up.

Fig 2

If a vehicle approaches you as you reach position 4, pull up and let the other vehicle pass, because of your position in the road and the potential danger involved, the other road user could pull up behind you, therefore you have no option but to return to position 2.

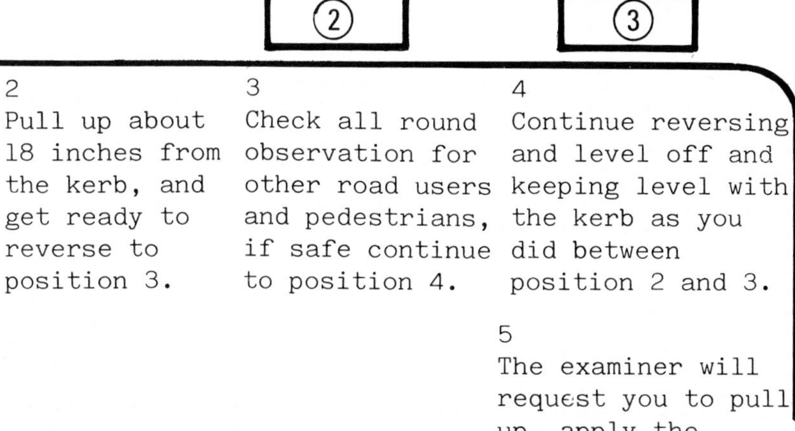

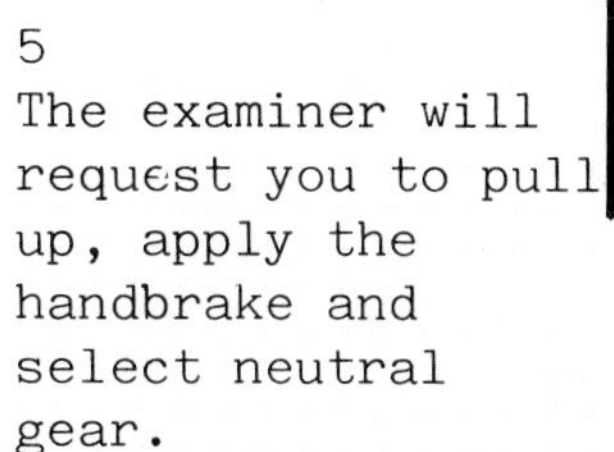

1
Pull up just before the corner as the examiner has requested. When the examiner tells you to move off when you are ready, move to position two.

2
Pull up about 18 inches from the kerb, and get ready to reverse to position 3.

3
Check all round observation for other road users and pedestrians, if safe continue to position 4.

4
Continue reversing and level off and keeping level with the kerb as you did between position 2 and 3.

5
The examiner will request you to pull up, apply the handbrake and select neutral gear.

Reverse into a limited opening to the left.

Top left:
You should position your vehicle so that it is parallel with and about 18in from the kerb before you pull up. When ready and safe to do so, reverse to Position Three.

Top right:
Reversing towards Position Three This is the view you will see as you look through the rear window, once you have got into a comfortable seating position to reverse towards the corner. You will be looking over your left shoulder and looking at where the kerb passes through the bottom of the rear window. At the same time be aware of any approaching traffic.

Bottom left:
Move off when safe to do so, keeping the kerb passing through the same point at the bottom of the rear window.

Bottom right:
Position Three Take note where the kerb passes through the rear window now. When safe to do so continue reversing keeping the kerb passing through the window as shown here.

Top left:
Position Four Half-way round the corner.

Far left:
Position Five As you leave Position Four, look at the bottom of the rear window as you did between Positions Two and Three, keeping the kerb in the same place as you reverse. Keep reversing until the examiner asks you to pull up.

Left:
Position Five When you pull up, this is the view you will have to the front. Comply with the examiner's instruction, making sure it is safe to do so. If you removed your seat belt to do this manoeuvre replace it before you select gear.

A Semi-Sharp Corner

Above:
The procedure for the first part of a semi-sharp corner is the same as any corner. Follow the kerb in the rear window until you reach Position Three.

Below:
Position Three When you see the kerb on the corner passing through the nearside quarter-light window, turn the steering wheel so that you follow the kerb in the same point of the side window until you lose the kerb at Position Four. Then level off and keep reversing as you did between Two and Three.

A Sharp 90° Corner

Above:
The procedure for the first part of a sharp corner is the same as the other types of corner up to between Position Two and Three. You are advised to pull up about 2-3ft from the kerb. This particularly applies if your vehicle has not got a good steering lock, as maximum use of the steering is needed on this type of corner.

Below:
Position Three When you see the kerb on the corner passing through the nearside quarter-light window (as shown), turn the steering wheel quickly to the left to full lock. Your road speed should be slow. When you reach Position Four start to level off and keep reversing as you did between Position Two and Three.

A semi-sharp corner

Reverse into a limited opening to the right

Those driving test candidates who will have to take their test in a commercial vehicle (van), caravanette, or minibus will be requested to reverse their vehicles into a limited opening to the right. This is because of the limited visibility to the rear of this type of vehicle, which makes it safer to reverse this way. The diagrammatic representation of this manoeuvre is shown in Fig 3.

Remember that 'Control' and 'Due Regard for Other Road Users' faults are the same for car and van.

As you drive along the examiner will ask you to pull up on the left, just before the road on the right (Position 1). Carry out your stopping procedure and pull up smoothly and safely, apply the handbrake and move the gear lever into neutral. Then put your hand back on the steering wheel and do not switch off the engine.

The examiner is now going to give you the instruction to reverse into the road on the right. He will say ***'That road on the right is the one I should like you to reverse into. Continue driving on the left until you are past it, move across to the right and stop, then back in and continue to drive in reverse gear well down the side road, keeping reasonably close to the right-hand kerb. Move off when you're ready, please'.*** Now is the time to get ready to move off. Make sure it

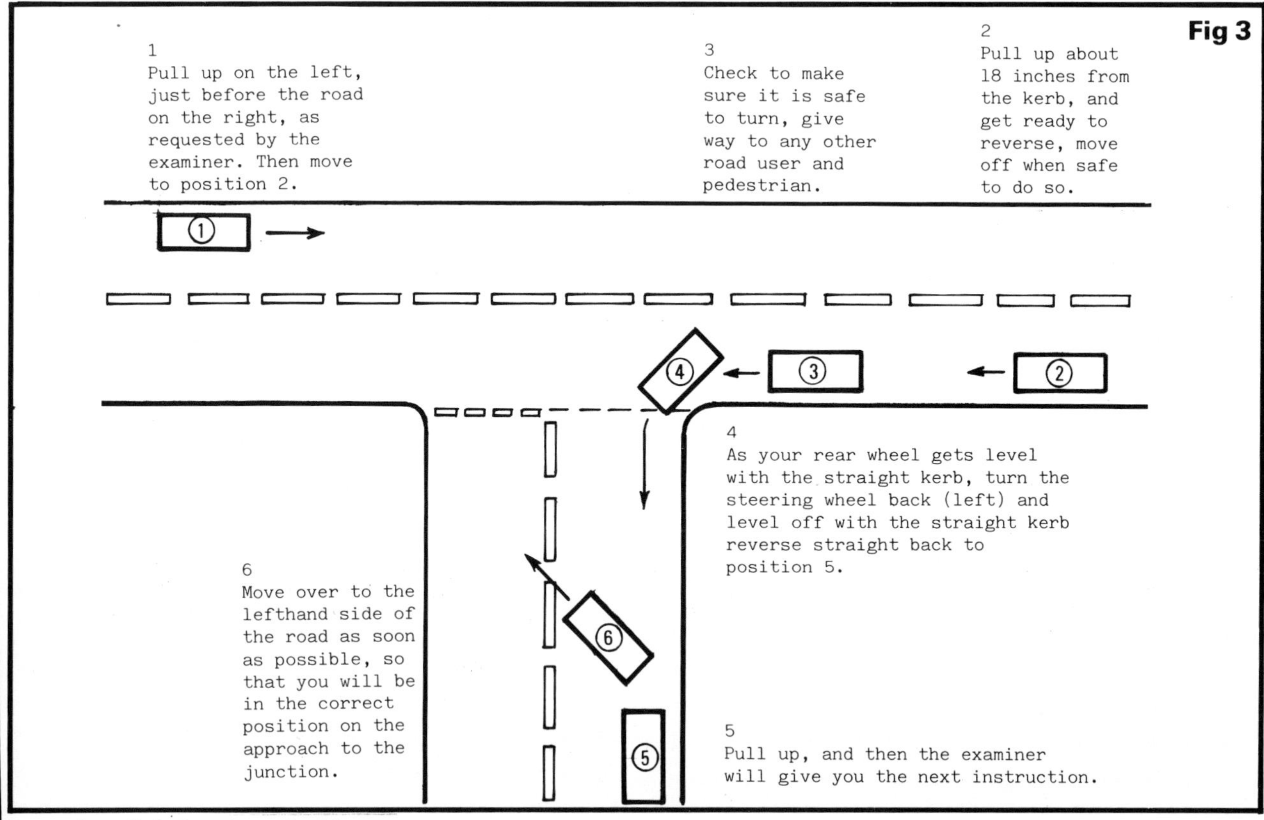

Reverse into a limited opening to the right.

is safe to do so by checking your mirrors and blind spot, and looking to the side road on the right for a vehicle which could be waiting to emerge. If clear, check the road ahead and if you are sure it is safe to move off, release the handbrake and move off smoothly. As soon as you move off, check your mirror and, if safe to do so, give a right turn signal by direction indicator. Check your mirror again and move to the crown of the road. As you get level with the side road on your right, look into it to make sure it will be clear and safe for you to reverse into. Check your mirror again and check the road ahead. If all is clear, move over to the right-hand side of the road and pull up about one vehicle length from the corner and about 12in from the kerb — Position 2. Apply the handbrake and move the gear lever into neutral.

Before you select reverse gear, open your window and move yourself into a position so that you can operate all the controls safely and be able to see the rear offside wheel in relation to the kerb. The accompanying photograph shows the position.

When you have got into a suitable seating position you can get ready to move off. Take all-round observation, and if the road is clear of traffic and there are no pedestrians who might be crossing, or about to cross, the road behind you, release the handbrake, put your hand back on the steering wheel and move your vehicle slowly backwards, maintaining the same distance from the kerb. Keep reversing slowly. Just before you reach the corner (Position 3), you must check all round you for other traffic and pedestrians. If in doubt, pull up and look all round. You cannot expect to do this exercise safely without proper observation and due regard to other road users. If the road ahead and behind you is clear, carry on reversing through Position 4 into the side road.

As you reverse down the side road, the vehicle must be 'under control' which means driven with reasonable accuracy and at a constant distance from the kerb. Continue well down the road so you will be in a safe position to move over to the left-hand side when you have completed this manoeuvre, and proceed to move off again toward the junction.

The examiner will ask you to pull up — Position 5. Do as requested and then apply the handbrake, move the gear lever into neutral and put your hand back on the steering wheel. The examiner will thank you and then ask you to move off when you are ready and at the end of the road turn right or left depending, of course, on the direction of the test route. Get ready to move off and take all-round observation, using the mirrors to their maximum advantage and looking through the vehicle to the rear, if possible. If clear give a left turn signal by direction indicator, check all round again and if clear release the handbrake, put your hand back on the steering wheel and move off smoothly to the left-hand side of the road — Position 6.

After you have levelled off, make sure your position in the road is correct for the direction you intend to go and that the signal is correct for your next turn.

Right:
Position One This is the position you should pull up at when the examiner requests you to do so — just before the road on the right.

Far right:
Position Two You should be one vehicle length from the corner and about 12in from the kerb, as shown here, and your vehicle should be parallel with the kerb.

Top left:
Position Two **Select a seating position so you can look out of your side window and still have full control of your vehicle.**

Bottom left:
Position Three **All-round observation must be checked before you start to turn. Make sure there are no pedestrians behind you – they could be in the blind area of your vehicle – and give way to any other vehicles. This driver is taking all-round observation before he starts to turn. Make sure you do too.**

Top right:
Position Four **Only when you have made sure it is safe to reverse do you continue round the corner. Note how the front of the vehicle swings out on the corner – this is why you must check your front for oncoming vehicles before turning. The amount of power you will need to perform this exercise safely will be determined by the camber of the road – especially at this point. To have the engine racing unnecessarily is a Control fault.**

Position Five **Is to reverse well down the side road, under control and with due regard for other road users.**

Bottom right:
Position Six **Move over to the left-hand side of the road well before the junction.**

Reversing Faults

Reversing Faults

Top left:
The learner has started to turn the steering wheel too late, and has gone wide round the corner. At the same time did not see an approaching vehicle, therefore it is a control and observation fault.

Bottom left:
Just before you reach the corner you must check the road behind you for pedestrians and other road users. This driver did not check the road behind him before he started to turn into the side road, did not see the pedestrian behind him and is going to cause danger to the pedestrian.

Top right:
This learner did not check to make sure it was safe to continue reversing into the side road, and did not see the approaching car. The front of his vehicle has swung out into the path of the approaching vehicle and has caused a dangerous situation to another road user.

Bottom right:
This learner has not checked the road behind before reversing into the side road, therefore has not seen the pedestrian crossing the road. Because of the lack of observation this fault has created a dangerous situation.

Top left:
This learner has started to turn the steering wheel too late, and has gone wide round the corner. This particular picture shows a Control fault.

Bottom left:
This candidate has started to turn the steering wheel too early and has mounted the pavement – another Control fault which can also be made in a van and which will be marked the same as a car.

Top right:
'With due regard for other road users' includes pedestrians – when reversing you must give way to any pedestrian who is crossing or is about to cross the road behind you. You must be aware of their presence.

Bottom right:
You must check to make sure it is safe to steer round the corner. Give way to any approaching traffic before turning round the corner.

Fig 4

(1)
When the examiner gives you the instruction to move off when you're ready, get ready to move off, check the mirror and blind spot, before releasing the handbrake. As soon as the vehicle moves, turn the steering wheel quickly.

(2)
As you reach 2 turn the steering wheel quickly to the left,

(4)
Start to turn the steering wheel quickly to the right.

(5)
Pull up and get ready to move off, then check to make sure it is safe to move off, before releasing handbrake.

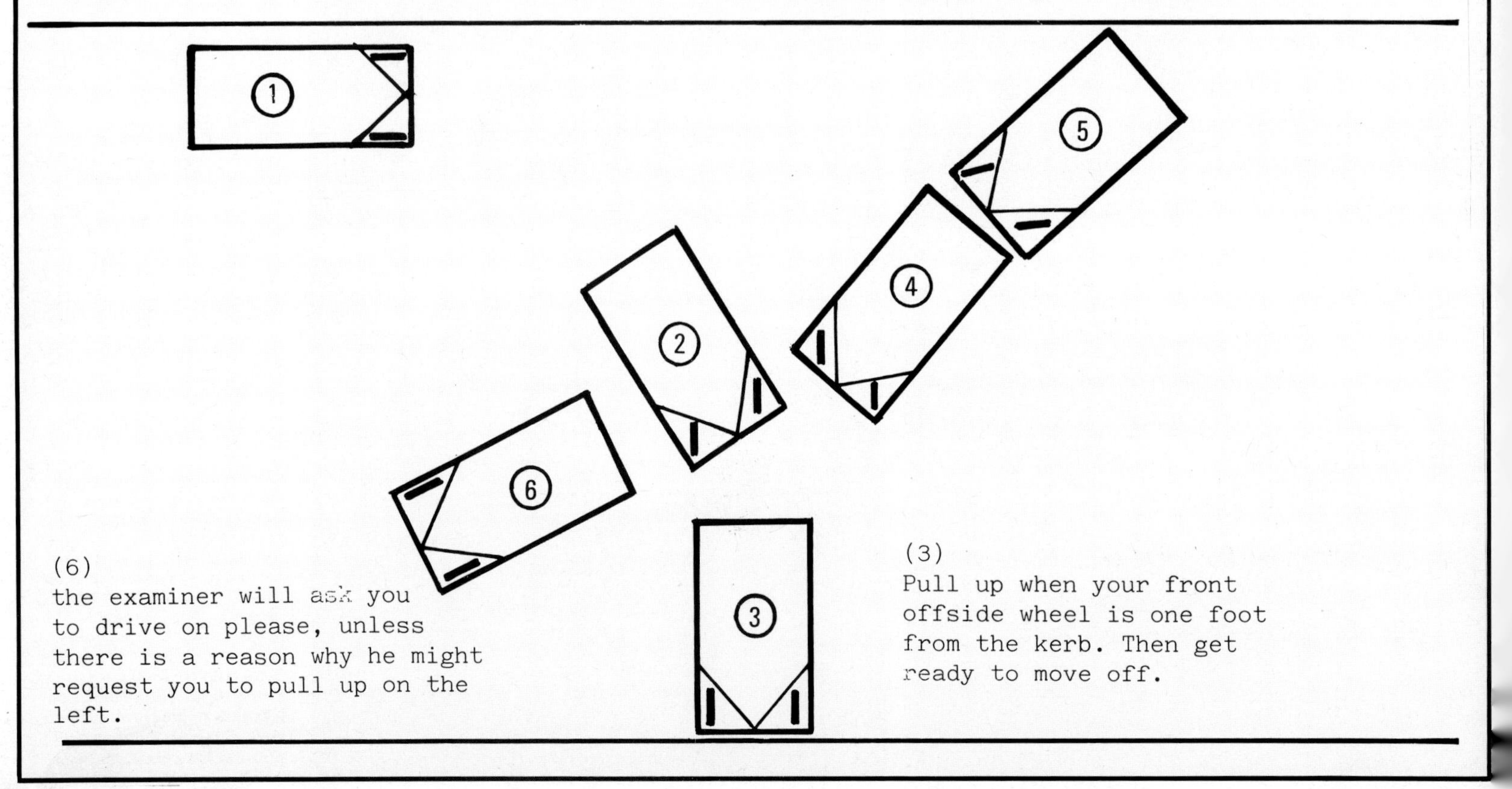

The turn in the road.

The Turn in the Road

Turn round by means of forward and reverse gears/under control/with due regard for other road users

After a few more minutes' driving you will soon be near to where you will do the next exercise — the turn round in the road. The purpose of this exercise is to show the examiner that you can handle your vehicle while manoeuvring it in a restricted space. At all times the vehicle must be under control and driven with due regard for other road users. Fig 4 gives a diagrammatic version of the turn in the road.

As you drive along the examiner will ask you to pull up on the left at a suitable place. Do not pull up near or opposite a hazard, such as a parked car or any other obstruction which could hinder you while manoeuvring your vehicle. When you pull up at a suitable place — Position 1 — apply the handbrake, move the gear lever into neutral and put your hand back on the steering wheel. The examiner will then give you the instructions for this exercise. He will say ***'I would like you to turn your car round to face the opposite way, using your forward and reverse gears. Try not to touch the kerb when you're turning. Move off when you're ready, please'.*** While the examiner is giving you the instruction for this exercise, take note of the camber of the road, as this will determine how much power you will need to move the vehicle, then get ready to move off. It is of the utmost importance that you take all-round observation before moving off. You should be looking for approaching traffic from either direction or pedestrians who could cross the road without warning. When clear, release the handbrake and move off slowly.

The procedure for turning in the road is outlined in the following photographs. Once completed the examiner will thank you and ask you to move off when you are ready.

Left:
Position One Get ready to move off, check your mirror and look round at the blind spot, road ahead and the pavement opposite. If clear, release the handbrake and move off slowly and smoothly. If in doubt WAIT. This driver is checking his blind spot. You can see by this example what could happen if you do not.

Top left:
Position Two **As you move slowly forward turn the steering wheel quickly to the right and look to your front offside. Don't rush this exercise. Keep control of your vehicle by careful use of the controls. When the front offside wheel is about 4ft from the kerb, keep your vehicle moving, but now turn the steering wheel quickly to the left, just as this driver is about to do.**

Above:
Position Three **Pull up when your front offside wheel is about 1ft from the kerb, apply the handbrake and select reverse gear. Look all round for traffic and pedestrians. If clear, get ready to move off. Look right, left and right again. If clear reverse slowly, turning the steering wheel quickly to the left, looking over your left shoulder as you reverse.**

Left:
Position Four **Note how this driver is looking over his left shoulder. When the rear off-side wheel is about 4ft from the kerb, turn the steering wheel quickly to the right, and at the same time look over your right shoulder.**

Far left:
Position Five   This driver is looking over his right shoulder at the kerb and for pedestrians while turning the steering wheel to the right. When the rear offside wheel is about 1ft (·3m) from the kerb, pull up, apply the handbrake and select first gear.

Left:
Look right, left and right again; when the road is clear of traffic get ready to move off. Then recheck your right, left and right again; if clear release the handbrake and move off slowly, turning the steering wheel quickly to the right as you move off.

Far left:
Position Six   As you level off with the kerb the examiner will ask you to drive on. If you removed your seat belt to do this manoeuvre, check your mirror, signal left if necessary, and pull up level with the kerb and carry out the procedure as mentioned earlier under cockpit drill. When you have put your seat belt on get ready to move off, check your mirror, blind spot and if clear release the handbrake and move off.

Left:
This driver is putting his seat belt on again before driving on. Don't forget yours.

Turn in the Road Faults

Turn in the Road Faults

Right:
The examiner did say 'try not to touch the kerb when you're turning'. This driver has touched the kerb, therefore will be marked for a Control fault.

Centre, top:
Because this driver misjudged the width of the road or lost control of his vehicle, danger has been created to a pedestrian on a footpath. For this fault the driver would not pass his test because of a dangerous Control fault.

Below right:
This driver did not make sure it was safe to reverse, and has done so without due regard for other road users, in this case pedestrians.

Far right, top
Do not turn the steering wheel while the vehicle is stationary.

Far right, bottom:
If a vehicle approaches — as in this situation — while your vehicle is in Position Three or Five, let it pass, unless the driver makes it obvious that you should proceed. If you let the vehicle pass, the handbrake should be applied and the engine should be running at tick-over speed as a safety precaution. Remember what the *Highway Code* states regarding flashing of headlamps by other drivers. Wait and let them pass.

Summary

It is illegal to park a vehicle within 15yd of a junction on its approach side, but it is permitted, as requested by the examiner, to pull up within this distance on the test so that the examiner can check the road he would like you to reverse into is clear. If clear, he will then give you the instruction for the reversing exercise.

When reversing round a corner do not keep the engine racing excessively and unnecessarily, as this is a control fault which could be potentially dangerous.

Make sure it is safe to reverse by looking all round before you start and just before the corner. If in doubt, wait.

Determine the type of corner you are going to reverse round and any camber before you start this exercise.

Before starting the turn round in the road, look at the camber of the road as this will influence how much power you will need to move off safely and under control. Take all-round observation to make sure it is safe to start this exercise.

While doing the turn round in the road do not race the engine excessively and unnecessarily as this is a control fault. The amount of forward and backward movement needed to turn your vehicle round to face the opposite way will be decided by the width of the road, the length of your vehicle, the steering lock on your vehicle and your competence in the way you use the controls.

Beware of pedestrians on the pavement, especially when you are reversing and your vehicle has a large overhang at the back, as this can be potentially dangerous. If in doubt wait and let them pass.

If a vehicle approaches you during the turn round in the road and you are between Positions 3 and 5, let the approaching vehicle pass unless the approaching driver makes it obvious that he is going to give you right of way for you to proceed safely.

If you take your seat belt off to do the reverse or turn in the road exercise, do not forget to put it on again once you have completed the exercise and your vehicle is stationary.

4 Mirrors, Signals, Road Signs and Speed

Mirrors

Make effective use of mirror(s) well before signalling/changing direction/slowing down/or stopping

Two of the most dangerous and common faults drivers make are misuse of the mirror or not using it at all. Some learner drivers try to exaggerate the use of the mirror to the examiner by excessive head or body movements — this practice can be very dangerous. The interior mirror should be adjusted so that only a head movement is needed to be able to look into it properly. It is perfectly possible to check the mirror with just an eye movement. This is classed as a glance, and is not good enough. To make proper and effective use of the mirror you have to move your head to look at it.

During the test the learner driver has to carry out certain procedures which lead to a number of systematic movements — like the system for approaching junctions and other hazards. The proper and effective use of the mirror is an essential part of the systems. If the driver does not carry out the sequence of movements as specified, then the system in question will be incomplete and the driver could be a danger to himself or other road users or pedestrians — and that means the candidate will not pass the test.

Right:
During a heavy shower the view to the rear can be obscured as shown here. Make sure it is safe to change course before doing so, otherwise a dangerous situation may occur.

Left:
Unless you look in the mirror(s) just before changing direction, you could be involved in a serious accident. Note the red car overtaking in a dangerous and wrong place.

Bottom:
If a vehicle is following you too closely, do not make any manoeuvre before making sure it is safe to do so. This can only be done by looking in the outside mirror where you will be able to see the road to the offside of the vehicle so close behind you.

Motorcyclists and cyclists attending a training scheme are given practical instruction on how to ride and control their machines properly, learning good roadcraft procedure. The effective and proper use of rear observation at the right time and place is part of good roadcraft and is vital to two-wheeled road users.

You have to know what vehicles are following you and what they are doing and the mirrors are the only source for this information. Sometimes, obviously, your view will be blocked — say by a large commercial vehicle. When this does happen it makes all your manoeuvres — like overtaking or turning — much more dangerous and you should be extremely cautious.

You must look in the mirror(s) well before signalling, changing direction, slowing down or stopping, otherwise you will not know if it is safe to do so.

Top left:
With a slight movement of the head — and a properly adjusted mirror — a driver will have a clear view of the road and traffic behind. A flat mirror will give you a more realistic idea of the distance of following traffic than a convex mirror.

Below left:
The car following this learner is too close — closer, indeed, than his stopping distance. This is a good example why you should know what is behind you at all times by making effective use of the mirror(s).

Top right:
Regardless of whether you have looked in the mirror and signalled correctly, there will always be some other road user who will take unnecessary chances like the driver who is overtaking this learner at a junction. Do not forget to look in the mirror before changing direction.

Bottom right:
This learner made effective use of the mirror before signalling and changing course. The mirrors must be used again before stopping.

Signals

Give signals/where necessary/correctly/in good time

There are three different types of visible signal fitted to every new car, the direction indicator signals, stoplamps and headlamps: the driver's arm signals make a fourth. These signals make up the language of the road and are the only ways drivers can inform other road users and pedestrians of their intentions and presence. If a signal is to be of any use, it must be given clearly, in good time and at the right time and place. By giving a signal, a driver is warning other road users that he intends to change course, slow down or stop. Too many serious accidents are caused by drivers and motorbike riders who signal their intention to carry out a manoeuvre and, without taking rear observation first, carried it out regardless of the position and speed of other road users following or overtaking them at the time. A signal *does not* give you the right of way: it gives no right whatsoever. A signal is a warning to other road users of the driver's intentions; no action should be taken unless it is safe to do so.

Direction Indicator Signals

The most common fault relating to signals is in their omission. Some drivers simply do not signal their intention to carry out a manoeuvre — this is particularly true when the road is clear of other road users and pedestrians. The proper use of signals is as much part of the various driving systems as is, for example, the use of the mirror. Without a signal the system is incomplete. Whether you have a clear road ahead or not, you must be able to demonstrate on the test that you know when and where to use a correct signal at the right time and place.

Some drivers give an incorrect signal, ie signal left when they intend to turn right, or signal right when they intend to turn left. The improper use of signals is dangerous and is the cause of many accidents. Some drivers do not even know their left from right, which is a poor excuse for displaying a wrong signal! It is the responsibility of every driver to familiarise himself with the controls and instruments of a vehicle before driving it.

The sole purpose of signalling is to let other road users and pedestrians know your intentions. If you signal late or too early, the signal will be useless and, in some situations, dangerous to pedestrians and other road users.

If you do not cancel your direction indicator signal after completing a manoeuvre and continue driving with the signal in

Left:
This 'L' driver is turning right, omitting to signal, therefore creating a potentially dangerous situation for the pedestrian and another road user.

operation, then you are guilty of improper use of signals. The indicator could be misleading and dangerous to other road users waiting to emerge at a junction, who could pull out in front of you. When you have completed a manoeuvre, check to make sure the direction indicator signal is cancelled.

The only arm signal required during a driving test is on the approach to a Zebra Crossing. The purpose of an arm signal is to inform pedestrians and any other traffic of your intention to slow down, stop and give way to pedestrians who are waiting to cross the road. The signal you give on the approach to the crossing must be given clearly and in good time so that other road users have adequate time to slow down and stop. All arm signals and direction indicator signals are illustrated in the *Highway Code* and your signals must be given as illustrated.

An arm signal can also be used when you have to slow down on the approach to a push-button controlled crossing or give way to any pedestrian who is on the crossing.

Headlamps

The primary function of the car's headlamps is, obviously, to light your way. However, they can also be used as a signal to warn of your presence. This can be very easily misunderstood, as it is common practice for some drivers to interpret a headlamp flash as an invitation for them to proceed or have right of way. A headlamp flash means the same as sounding the horn: it is to let other road users know of your presence and for no other reason.

Stoplamps

The stoplamps are fitted to the rear of your vehicle and are illuminated when the brake pedal is pressed. This signal is useful in letting vehicles behind you know that you are slowing down, but it must be appreciated that the stoplamps do not illuminate until the brake pedal has been pressed. You could well have started to slow down before the lamps illuminate. The use of the mirror before braking is a very important factor as you must know what is behind you before you brake. Brake smoothly in good time, and then following traffic will have time to act on the signal you are giving.

Horn

The other type of signal fitted to your vehicle is an audible one — the horn. The purpose of this is to attract the attention of another road user, cyclist or pedestrian, particularly children, after every other precaution has been taken. The horn should only be sounded when it is really necessary — as a last resort to warn of your presence other road users and pedestrians, who otherwise might not have seen you.

Signals Omitted

The correct use of signals is part of good driving. It is important that other road users and pedestrians know in good time what your intentions are. This selection of photographs shows examples of signal faults which can be committed during the driving test and which will result in a failure.

Right:
This driver is going to turn left without a signal, therefore creating a potentially dangerous situation for another road user.

Far right:
This driver has created a dangerous situation because he omitted to signal his intention to turn left, therefore creating a dangerous situation for the pedestrian.

Give Signals Correctly

Top left:
This 'L' driver has created a potentially dangerous situation to another road user because he has not signalled his intention to turn right.

Bottom left:
When approaching a zebra crossing with pedestrians on it or about to cross, signal in good time your intentions to slow down or stop. Your signal will assist other road users to take the appropriate action. Allow extra stopping distance when the road is wet or slippery. This driver has got his window up and is therefore unable to give an arm signal which is a fault for signal omitted.

Give Signals Correctly

Top right:
If a vehicle is parked just before the road into which you are going to turn, position your vehicle in good time and then signal your intention to turn left. In this situation the driver is in the correct position in the road to signal left.

Bottom right:
This driver has signalled left too early, because he is in the wrong position in the road to signal, due to the parked vehicle. A change of course — to the right — will have to be made, creating potential danger to following traffic because of the wrong signal.

Above right:
In this situation the 'L' driver should have signalled his intention to pull up as he was level with the other road user waiting to emerge: because he has signalled too soon the other road user could have pulled out in front of the learner.

Above far right:
This 'L' driver has signalled too late, his intention to turn right, therefore creating potential danger to another road user.

Right:
Never signal pedestrians to leave a pavement or central refuge as this will put them in danger from other road users.

Give Signals in Good Time

Road Signs

Take prompt and appropriate action on all/traffic signs/road markings/traffic lights/ signals given by traffic controllers/other road users

Traffic signs, road markings, signals given by traffic controllers and other road users are the language of the road. To gain maximum benefit from the information given by the signs and signals, you must look well ahead with complete concentration. Only then will you receive the messages in time to assess the situation and act on the information. You will then be able to act appropriately and correctly at the right place. This also applies to signals given by other road users and traffic controllers, such as police officers in uniform, traffic wardens and a school crossing patrol. This selection of photographs shows various signs and signals which can be seen when driving — and some of the mistakes that you can make through misinterpretation or faulty action.

Give Signals in Good Time

Top left:
This driver signalled his intention to turn right too late, which could have caused a danger for another road user.

Bottom left:
This driver signalled to turn left too late. He started indicating only a short distance from the road he wanted to join. Because he signalled too late he has created potential danger to another road user.

Bottom:
If you do not comply with a 'Stop' sign you will commit an offence and will not pass the test.

Direction Signs

Direction Signs

Right:

If you do not comply with a 'Give Way' sign you cause potential danger or inconvenience to another road user or pedestrian who may be on the road that you are going to cross or join so you will not pass the test.

Far right:

If you have an obstruction on your side of the road — like roadworks on a bend where your vision is obscured, proceed slowly and be prepared to stop. The vehicle should be driven at a speed at which it can be stopped within the distance the driver can see to be clear. Do not be like some drivers who stubbornly go through a gap, forcing oncoming drivers to slow down or stop.

Tree cutting

Top:
Roadside markers are black and white posts with oblong amber reflectors. These markers give the same warning as a black and white chevron sign. When you see them reduce speed on the approach to a bend.

Below right:
The examiner will not give a directional instruction when there are directional signs. If a test candidate has to ask which way they should go, and some do, they will not pass the test.

Far right:
In some towns there are pre-warning directional signs of lane markings ahead. Use the information they give you, otherwise you will be in the wrong lane when you reach the junction ahead. For one reason best known to himself, this test candidate is going to turn right when the traffic sign directs him left. This type of fault does occur and results in failure of the test.

Top left:
This driver is going to make a prohibited right turn and will fail the test for doing so.

Above:
The 'No Entry' sign is self-explanatory. If you do not comply with this sign you will break the law and will not pass the test.

Left:
It is important that you position your vehicle in the correct lane in good time for the direction you intend to go. If you do not you could create a potentially dangerous situation.

Above right:
If you do not take the necessary action on the information given by warning signs you could create a dangerous situation.

Right:
Slow down in good time so that you do not endanger the workmen or other road users to which the road sign referred.

Road Markings

Road Markings

Top left:
It is important that you are in the correct lane on the approach to a junction, using the appropriate direction indicator signal for the direction that you are going to travel.

Bottom left:
Take extra care as you approach a double roundabout with numerous road markings. Look well ahead so as to give yourself ample time to plan your actions.

Top right:
You should be in the correct lane for the direction you intend to travel.

Bottom right:
If there are road works or other obstructions on the approach to a roundabout, you must reduce speed so you can stop and give way to traffic leaving the roundabout. In this situation you will be joining the roundabout from the wrong side of the road, therefore look to your right in good time.

School
DEPT. OF TRANSPORT
APPROVED DRIVING INST.
F41 GNM

Far left:
This driver is going to turn right. His position in the road is wrong because he has crossed a hazard line when it was not safe to do so, therefore creating a potentially dangerous situation for a motorcyclist.

Above left:
Some roads have areas which have white diagonal stripes or white chevrons painted on them. This has been done to separate traffic streams which could be a danger to each other. It also protects traffic when turning right. Keep off the marked area if it is safe to do so.

Below left:
This learner is in the correct lane for turning right. All unwanted road speed should be lost in the lane designated for turning right, as shown here, and not in the nearside lane where you will hinder other road users who are following the road ahead.

Below right:
This driver has positioned his vehicle for turning right too early and has therefore not complied with the *Highway Code*.

Top:
Do not enter a box junction unless your exit is clear. (Read the relevant section in the *Highway Code*.)

Bottom:
In some areas as you get near a school you will see a flashing amber signal below the advance sign which warns of a school crossing patrol operating ahead. Look in the mirror and adjust your speed and drive slowly near schools where children could run out suddenly.

Traffic Light Signals

Traffic Light Signals

Top:
A traffic light signal showing red means 'stop'. If you do not comply with this signal you will create a dangerous situation. You must comply with the traffic light signals as shown in the *Highway Code*.

Bottom:
A traffic light signal showing a green light means you may proceed if the way is clear. Special care is needed if you intend to turn left or right and give way to pedestrians who are crossing. You must anticipate the traffic signals changing to red as you approach. If you do not you will create a potentially dangerous situation.

Traffic Controllers

Far left:

If the traffic signals are not working, treat and approach the junction like an uncontrolled junction. Nobody has the right of way. Make sure it is safe for you to emerge into the junction. If in doubt, wait.

Traffic Controllers

Far left:

You must comply with any signal given by a Police Officer in uniform.

Above centre:

You must stop when requested to do so regardless of whether the road ahead looks clear.

Above right:

You must obey a signal given by a Traffic Warden.

Left:

You must stop when signalled to do so by a school crossing patrol exhibiting a 'STOP-CHILDREN' sign.

Signals by Other Road Users

Speed

Exercise proper care in the use of speed

Throughout the test you must keep within the speed limits as indicated by the traffic signs. If you break the law by exceeding the speed limit, or drive at an excessive speed at the wrong time or place, therefore causing potential danger to other road users or pedestrians, you will not pass the test.

Always drive at a speed so that you can pull up in the distance you can see to be clear.

In urban areas, the 30mph speed limit applies to roads which have lamp-posts within 200yd of each other and which have no repeater speed limit signs attached to them.

In rural areas some test routes include country roads and which have no footpaths (pavement). Be extra careful on the approach to a left-hand bend, where you could expect to meet pedestrians, cattle and animals being led on your side of the road.

Signals by Other Road Users

Above right:
This learner is signalling to turn right and braking. You must take prompt and appropriate action on signals given by other road users.

Right:
Be aware of animals and act accordingly to any signal given by the rider or person in charge.

Far right:
Do not exceed the official speed limit regardless of whether you have a clear road ahead of you.

Above:
Whenever daytime visibility is seriously reduced by mist or smoke, or traffic conditions, keep your speed down so that you can stop well within the distance you can see to be clear. Use the headlamps with the beam dipped so that you can see and be seen.

Left:
When approaching animals reduce speed. Do not rev the engine or drive too fast, too close or sound your horn. Allow adequate clearance as you pass, otherwise you could create a potentially dangerous situation for the horse and rider.

Above right:
The speed limit in this road is 30mph, but to attempt to drive at 30mph would be dangerous because of the prevailing conditions. You must exercise proper care in the use of speed at all times and drive at a speed which is suitable for the conditions prevailing.

Right:
Look well ahead and be prepared to slow down and stop when and where the situation demands. You cannot do this if you drive at an excessive speed at the wrong time and place.

Far right:
When you have passed the loose chippings make normal progress if safe to do so.

Make progress by driving at a speed appropriate to the road and traffic conditions/ avoiding undue hesitancy

It is important that you make progress throughout your test by driving at a speed appropriate to the road and traffic conditions at the time. If you drive at a speed which is well below that which is permitted – assuming that the traffic conditions and state of the road do not warrant a speed reduction – you could create a potentially dangerous situation.

Another example of 'undue hesitancy' can be seen at the approach to a junction. If you apply the system as specified in Chapter 5 and see that the road is clear well to the right and left of you, but nevertheless pull up at the junction and do not take advantage of the opportunity to move off when it is clear and safe for you to do so, you could well hold up traffic behind you and create a potentially dangerous situation.

Summary

When you look in the mirror, do not just look at what you see, make effective use and act sensibly on what you see in good time.

Never start a manoeuvre without first looking in the mirror.

Do not give any signal too early as it could confuse other road users. Do not signal too late because a late signal provides useless information. Both these faults could be potentially dangerous. Give the correct signal for the direction you intend to go and do not forget to cancel the signal after you have completed the manoeuvre.

There is one arm signal which you must use if needed during the test and that is a slowing down signal as you approach a Zebra Crossing.

Look well ahead for traffic signs and road markings and take the appropriate action indicated by the signs and markings in good time where practically possible.

Do not drive at an excessive speed at the wrong time or place. But do not over-compensate – you will not pass the test if you drive at a crawling pace. Make progress as appropriate to the road and traffic conditions and avoid undue hesitancy. Look well ahead and plan your driving on what you can and cannot see to be clear.

Do not use one signal for two different manoeuvres.

Do not slow down too early on the approach to a junction and then have to use the accelerator to gain speed to take you up to the junction. This is a common fault for not making progress appropriate to the road and traffic conditions.

Above:
With a clear road ahead you should make progress by driving at a speed appropriate to the traffic conditions.

Left:
This driver has a clear road ahead and to his right, but has pulled up when there is no need to do so which can create a potentially dangerous situation.

5 Junctions

Act Properly at Road Junctions

A junction, whatever its type, is a hazard, potentially dangerous in itself. It must be approached with caution. The only way this can be done with complete control and safety, is to carry out systematically a number of movements in sequence over a given distance. To achieve this satisfactorily you must give maximum concentration to your driving and observations: this way a correct assessment can be made and enable you to act properly at road junctions. You must recognise any situation or hazard in good time, so you will be able to take the appropriate action, ie change course or slow down. On the approach to any junction or hazard, never assume that another road user or pedestrian will react correctly at any given moment, otherwise a dangerous situation could develop.

If carried out smoothly and systematically the system outlined below leaves nothing to chance and can be applied to any hazard.

The examiner will give you directional instructions in good time, which will give you time to carry out the manoeuvres. You will be marked on the report sheet if you miss any movements of the system. The phrases the examiner will use for directing you over the test route are as follows:

To take the first road: *'take the next road on the right/left, please'*. To take the second road: *'will you take the second road on the right/left, please'* (if there is likely to be any doubt, the examiner will say ***'this is the first'*** as you approach it).

Turning at the junction: *'At the end of the road turn right/left, please'*. As you approach a roundabout: *'at the roundabout take the next road off to the left, please'*. Turning right: *'at the roundabout take the road leading off to the right, please'* and straight ahead, *'at the roundabout follow the road ahead, please'*. If you approach a roundabout which has more than four exits, the examiner will make it clear to you which exit he would like you to take.

Before examining the step-by-step sequence in detail, there are various points about junctions worthy of further detail. To begin with, as you approach a junction, you must assess what you see — what type of junction it is (T, crossroads, roundabout etc) and how dense the traffic is. Your speed on the approach must be considered so that you can give yourself time to act should something unexpected happen.

As you approach a junction you should be able to see clearly into the road you are going to join or cross. If for one reason or another it is not possible to do so, you should move your vehicle slowly forward so that you will be in a position to look right, left and right again, to make sure whether it is safe to proceed or not. If in doubt, wait.

Effective observation before emerging from a junction is terribly important. A driver, when sitting in a normal driving position in a saloon car, will on average have a view of about 4ft from the ground of the road ahead, to the rear and to either side. Therefore any objects in the vicinity which are above 4ft high will hide potential danger.

A driver's zone of vision on the approach to and at a junction can be obscured by many things — street furniture like lamp-posts, keep-left bollards on a central refuge, traffic signs and other fixtures such as railings, telegraph poles, postboxes, hedges and shrubs. Even a pedestrian walking on the pavement can obscure your view of the road which you are going to join.

There are certain parts of a vehicle's bodywork that also obstruct a driver's view — roof supports, door pillars, etc force you to move your head or body to gain a better and unrestricted view of the road that you want to join.

The weather too can impair vision from inside a car — if you do not keep your vehicle well ventilated on a cold or wet day the windows will mist up and greatly reduce your all-round vision. Some drivers make no conscious effort to improve the situation which is lazy and dangerous. On the other hand, on a sunny day, the windows will be clear but you could have the sun shining in your eyes. Here the use of the sun visor or sun-glasses will help reduce the glare.

Left:
The learner pulls up at the junction and gets ready to move off. The road to his left is clear, but a van is approaching from his right and is signalling with its left-hand direction indicator. Assuming the van is going to turn left the learner driver releases the handbrake and starts to move forward slowly.

Whatever the circumstances are at a junction, the most important thing is to act sensibly on what you can and cannot see to be clear. Some test candidates look right, left and right again on the approach or at a junction and emerge straight into the path of an approaching vehicle. The reason they take this dangerous action is because they did not make effective use of what they saw, or did not take appropriate action, ie to wait at the junction until it was safe to emerge into the road. Do not assume anything at a junction until you are completely sure it is safe to proceed. Carry out the sequence outlined and when you are completely sure that you will not create any inconvenience or potential danger to any other road user or pedestrian should you proceed. If in doubt, wait.

Acting properly at a junction is a very important part of the driving test and one of the highest percentage factors which contributes to the failure of a candidate on the test is incorrect observation during this manoeuvre. Many learners and, indeed, qualified drivers, either look too early or too late as they approach a junction. If they look too early they are sometimes in the wrong position to be able to see what vehicles are approaching, because their visibility on the approach to junctions can be very limited. At the other extreme, if they look too late, they see things but are too late to act on the information.

Even when the observation takes place at the right time some learners, through inexperience, underestimate the speed and distance of an approaching vehicle. Some novice drivers are under the impression that the smaller the approaching vehicle is, the farther away it must be. To some extent this is true — but not always. A classic example of this is the motorcycle. Motorbikes are a third the size of a saloon car which is why there are so many bike-related accidents at junctions. The average driver is looking for other cars and commercial vehicles, but on many occasions miss the approaching motorcyclist. The accompanying photographs show a typical sequence of events that could so easily happen if care is not taken.

Above right:
The van is still signalling and begins to reduce speed so that the turn can be made safely. The road to the learner's left is still clear of traffic.

Right:
The van driver starts to steer the van round the corner, the learner moves farther forward into the junction.

THINK BIKE before emerging

Motorcycles and mopeds are much faster today than before. Do not underestimate the speed and distance of an approaching motorcyclist: many drivers have done and in consequence emerged from junctions causing serious injury or caused a fatal accident.

Not all motorcyclists help make themselves more visible to drivers by wearing brightly coloured clothing or belts or tabards which provide fluorescent daytime brightness and night-time reflective brilliance. Indeed some cyclists do not even drive with their headlights on during daylight hours.

Motorcyclists are much more open to the elements, dangerous road surfaces and other potential dangers than car drivers. Some drivers do not appreciate or are not even aware of these problems. In Chapter 2 it was explained how the different types of road surfaces and other deciding factors can affect and determine the overall stopping distance of a vehicle at a given speed. Motorcycles and mopeds take a greater distance to stop than a saloon car or van, even more so in adverse weather conditions and on inferior road surfaces.

It must be appreciated that the overall size of a motorcyclist and motorcycle is about one-third of the size of a car — easily

Left:
As the rear of the van gets level with the learner a motorcyclist appears. The learner brakes hard.

Bottom left:
The moped rider is now on a collision course with the learner. Never assume that a vehicle is going to turn at a junction, even though a signal is being displayed. Wait to make sure there is no other road user behind the approaching vehicle before you move off.

Below:
Can you see a motorcyclist approaching? Think bike before emerging.

missed if effective observation is not taken and easily hit if effective action is not taken once it has been noticed.

It is your responsibility as a driver to see and estimate the speed and distance of an approaching motorcyclist or other road users before deciding to emerge into a junction.

The Government legislated on motorcycles in 1982 and from 29 March of that year learner motorcycle and scooter drivers were restricted to a machine of 125cc which had an engine with a maximum power output of 12bhp. There was a two-part motorcycle test and a restriction on the length of time a novice rider could hold a Group D provisional licence.

The Government produced the legislation as a safety package for novice riders. New legislation has now taken place. The need to pass a test provides an important incentive for proper training and therefore could produce safe motorcyclists aware of their commitment to their own and other road users' and pedestrians' safety.

The Government is still trying to reduce accidents involving the two-wheeled road user: make sure you make your contribution by looking out for motorcyclists or cyclists at junctions. If you pull out in front of a motorcyclist or cyclist it could be someone you know who is about to be injured.

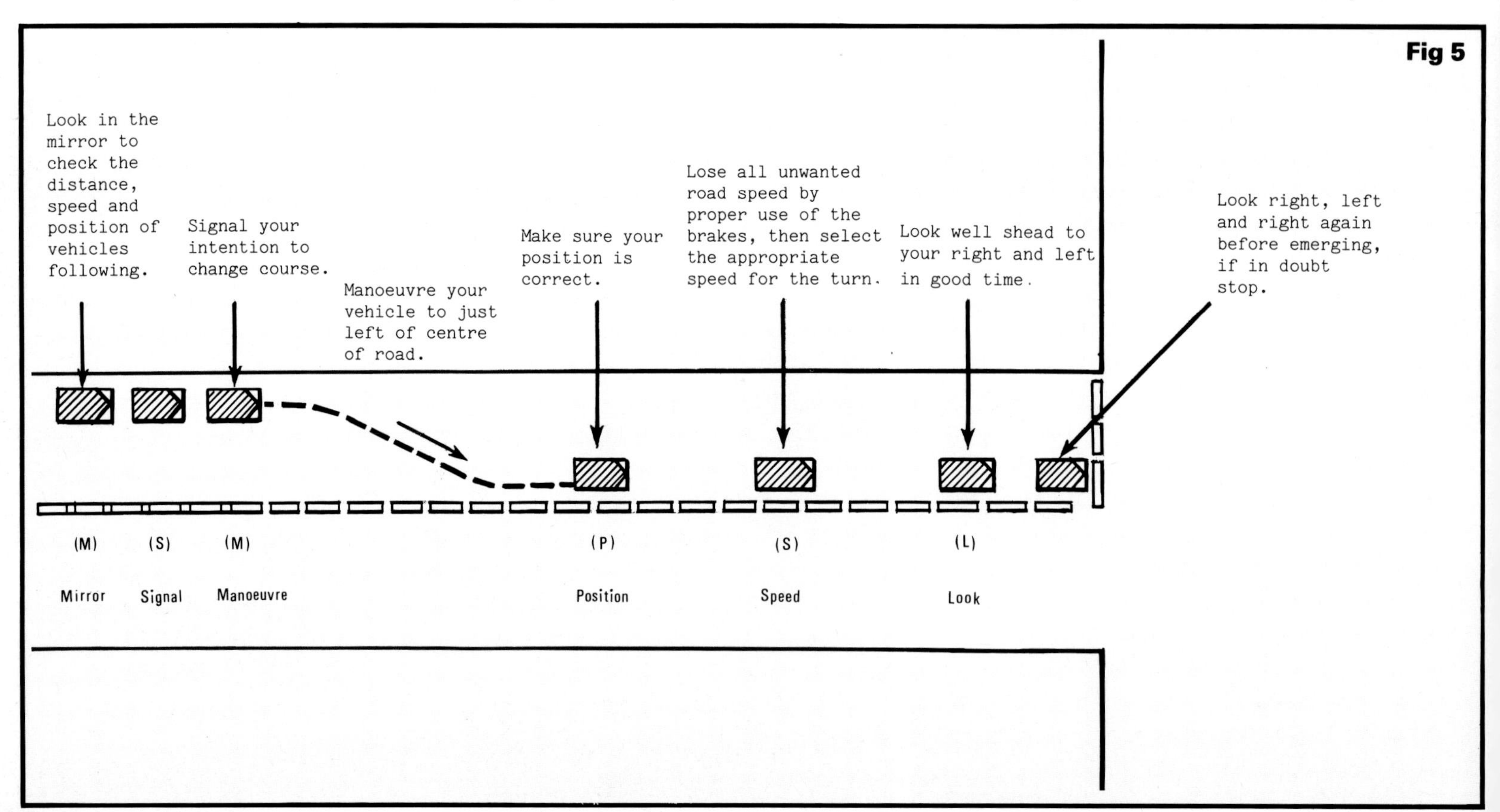

Turning right at a crossroads.

The System for a Right Turn at a Crossroads

We shall now examine the step-by-step sequence of events that should occur on the approach to a junction, using the difficult right turn at a crossroads as an example.

The examiner will give you a directional instruction in good time, so that well before reaching the crossroads your road observation should have assessed the junction and you should have formulated a safe driving plan. In this example your assessment of the junction informs you of a crossroads with a 'Give Way' sign and road markings. There is a limited zone of vision to the right caused by tall hedges.

As soon as the examiner gives you the instructions the following sequence of movements should take place:

1. Look in the mirror to see what traffic is behind you, how close it is and what it is doing.
2. Signal your intention to change course, providing it is safe to do so.
3. Look in the mirror again to make sure it is safe to change course to the crown of the road. If safe to do so, steer a steady course to the crown of the road. Do not swerve or turn the steering wheel in jerky movements while changing course.
4. Check your position in the road. The offside wheels should be just to the left of the centre of the road. The hazard lines ahead of you will be a good guide.
5. Check again in the mirror before applying the footbrake.
6. Brake gently on the approach to the junction.
7. Observation coming up to the junction – look right, left, right to check.
8. If safe to do so, select a suitable gear and move in the direction required. If it is not safe to continue, check in your mirror and brake gently to a halt at the junction. Apply the handbrake and wait for a safe gap in the traffic before turning.

The accompanying photographs show visually this step-by-step sequence.

Top:
Movement One – Mirror
Look in the mirror to see what traffic is behind you.

Middle:
Movement Two – Signal
Signal your intention to change course by using a direction indicator signal providing it is safe to do so.

Bottom:
Movement Three – Mirror
Look in the mirror to check if it is safe to change course. If safe to do so, move out to the crown of the road.

Top left:
The next stages are carried out in close sequence. Movement Four — Position Check your position. The ideal course is just left of the centre of the road, provided it is safe to do so.

Top right:
Movement Five — Mirror, Signal, Speed. The mirrors must be used again to check for traffic. The signal should be checked to ensure it has not cancelled itself. The position of any following traffic must be considered when your speed is being reduced through proper use of the gears.

Bottom left:
Movement Six — Observation. Look to the right as soon as it is possible. In doing so an assessment can be made of what can and cannot be seen to be clear.

Bottom right:
Movement Seven — Observation. Once you have looked to the right, you should look to the left for any approaching traffic. If clear, look to the right again.

Top:
Movement Eight — Give Way. Traffic can be seen approaching from the right. Use the mirrors again. Apply the footbrake so that the vehicle stops at the correct place.

Bottom:
Movement Nine — Move Off. When approaching traffic has passed, look to the front, right, left and right again. When you are satisfied it is safe to proceed, the handbrake should be released and the manoeuvre completed.

Act Properly at Junctions

The following examples are typical everyday situations and show how easy it is to miss another road user if effective observation is not taken. Drivers who glance, and many do, instead of looking right, left and right again, are dangerous and are likely to cause accidents. This type of driver will not pass the test.

Top left:
Within one second this moped will be obscured by the windscreen pillar.

Top right:
The majority of drivers look to their left but this rider is more to the front. If the driver should emerge into the junction an accident would occur.

Bottom left:
This car is partially hidden by the windscreen pillar.

Bottom right:
Can you see the moped which is only a few seconds away?

Far right:
Be extra careful when you emerge into a road that has a higher-than-average speed limit. Any obstacle that obstructs your view of the road, like this wall, is an additional hazard which can obscure your view of approaching traffic.

TO LET

Top left:
Where there are railings on the approach to a junction, look as early as practically possible, so you will be able to see through the railings for approaching traffic.

Top right:
If you look late, the railings will, at a certain angle, be like a solid wall which will obstruct your vision — as shown in this picture.

Right:
Take advantage of the windows in shops and houses as they can reflect the approach of another road user who cannot be seen from your position in the road. Can you see a car approaching?

Top left:
Traffic signs can obstruct your view of approaching traffic, like this example.

Left:
Parked vehicles can obstruct your view to either side. Move forward slowly until you can clearly see either side; be prepared to stop.

Bottom left:
If you pull up at the wrong place this will be your view. If possible try to pull up where you can see any approaching traffic.

Below:
Providing it is safe to do so, avoid stopping where your vision might be obscured, like in this situation.

Top left:
Pedestrians on a footpath can obstruct your view of the road. Can you see an approaching vehicle?

Bottom left:
It is crucial that you check to ensure your exit road on a roundabout is clear. In this situation roadworks are in progress, therefore any approaching traffic from the left will meet you on your side of the road, at your point of exit.

Top right:
This driver looked right, left and right again but underestimated the speed or distance of the approaching vehicle and emerged into the junction with dangerous results. Both drivers will have to brake hard to avoid a collision.

Bottom right:
If this driver had taken effective observation he would have seen the cyclist approaching. He did not; therefore the cyclist has had to swerve to avoid an accident.

The System for Going Straight Ahead at a Crossroads

This is very similar to that used for turning right but, because one is not changing lane, is somewhat simpler. As we said earlier, well before reaching the junction your observation will have allowed you to assess the junction ahead and formulate a safe driving plan. The sequence of movements starts in the same way as before. First, look in the mirror to see what traffic is behind you, how close it is and what it is doing. As you intend to go straight ahead, there should be no need to indicate a course alteration although you should position your vehicle correctly for the approach. Subject to there being no stationary vehicles in your path, you will then be on the correct course for the junction. If there are any vehicles parked on the approach to the junction, try to avoid using a moving out signal — unless absolutely necessary — as this could confuse or mislead other road users about your true intentions — ie they could think you intend to turn at the junction. If you do have to signal to change course, cancel the indicator as soon as practicably possible. Next, you must look in the mirror again because you are now going to adjust the speed of your vehicle by proper use of the footbrake. Having done so, select the appropriate gear and look right, left and right again and, if needed, check again. If you are sure you can emerge into the junction without creating any potential danger, then proceed.

Position the Vehicle Correctly Before Turning Right

As with the right turn at a crossroads, turning right into a side road is a difficult and potentially dangerous manoeuvre. It is of the utmost importance that you carefully apply all the steps in the system where practicably possible throughout your approach to the hazard.

As noted at the beginning of this chapter, the examiner will give you directional instruction in good time. However, an aware driver will have noticed the road configuration before the examiner speaks.

Consistent observation of movements of other traffic and pedestrians is vital and the ability to act quickly to any sudden changes is essential.

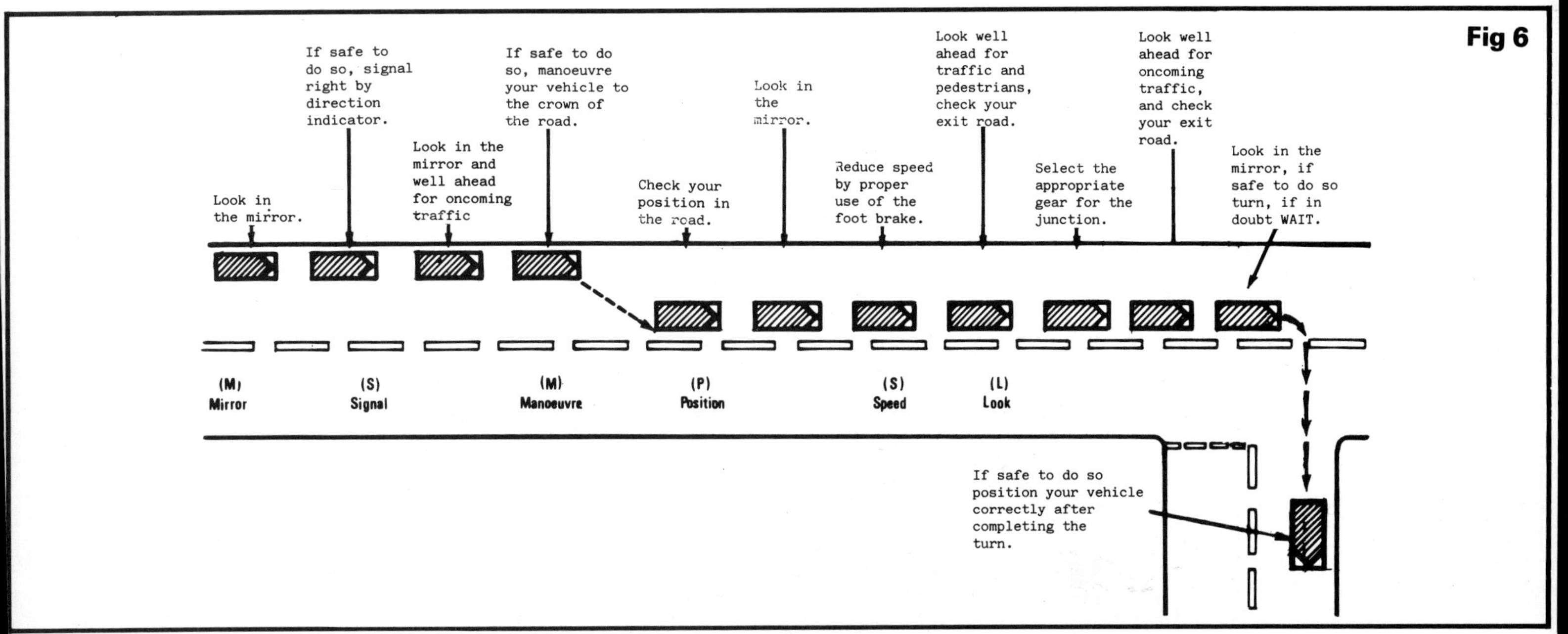

Turning right.

Top left:
This vehicle is in the correct position in the road for turning right. The last movement of the system here is to look well ahead for oncoming traffic. If clear, check the road you are going to turn into. If clear, look in the mirror before changing direction. If all clear turn on the correct course as previously mentioned.

Top right:
You must anticipate the length of other vehicles as you approach a junction — for instance a bus or heavy goods vehicle which has to cut the corner due to its length and the width of the road. Hold back in these circumstances and let them pass.

Bottom left:
Because of the approaching vehicle and the parked car, this learner has created a potentially dangerous situation because he positioned his vehicle to turn right too early.

Bottom right:
If there are parked vehicles on the approach and near the junction, slow down and give yourself time to position your vehicle correctly for turning right, like this driver.

Far right:
If you approach a junction too fast you will not give yourself time to position your vehicle correctly and, like this driver, could create a potentially dangerous situation because of the incorrect positioning.

DEPT. OF TRANSPORT
APPROVED DRIVING INST.
L
F75 GNM
F387 RLL

Junctions with Traffic Lights

Top left:
This driver has positioned his vehicle too far to the left and therefore is in an incorrect position for turning right.

Bottom left:
This driver has gone over the hazard line, creating potential danger to another road user.

Turning Right at a Junction Controlled by Traffic Lights

Top right:
The conventional way to turn right at a crossroad is to pass oncoming traffic so that the off-side of your vehicles are passing each other. Do not enter the junction if you will block the exit of an approaching vehicle.

Bottom right:
In some towns there are junctions which have lane markings directing you to turn so that you will be passing nearside to nearside. Be extra careful because your view of oncoming traffic can be restricted by a large vehicle. Like any other junction, do not proceed unless you can see the road is clear to do so.

Far top right:
Do not proceed if the road ahead is not clear and therefore unsafe.

Far bottom right:
This pre-warning sign is self-explanatory.

Avoid cutting right-hand corners

When turning right be particularly careful that you do not turn too early, otherwise you will cut the corner. This is especially dangerous because you will be on the wrong side of the road into which you are turning. This of course will endanger any traffic approaching the junction. Your vision on the approach to some junctions could be restricted by many different objects, ie buildings, tall hedges, parked vehicles, so that you will not be able to see into the road before you actually start to turn into it. Apart from being dangerous, the practice of cutting right-hand corners is bad, lazy driving.

Below:

This driver has cut a right-hand corner and by doing so has forced another motorist to take evasive action, by braking hard to avoid a collision.

Roundabouts

As with any other junction, it is of the utmost importance that you use your powers of observation to maximum advantage when approaching a roundabout.

The directional instructions the examiner will give you on the approach to a roundabout are **for turning left**, 'At the roundabout take the next road off to the left, please', **for turning right**, 'At the roundabout take the road leading off to the right, please'. **For straight ahead**, 'At the roundabout follow the road ahead, please'.

As you approach a roundabout the examiner will give you a directional instruction in good time. As soon as you have been given the instruction start the system if practicably possible.

Like any other junction you must look right, left and right again on the approach to a roundabout.

Top:
It is of the utmost importance that you position your vehicle in the correct lane, at the right time if possible, for the direction you intend to go and that you signal your intention as appropriate, by direction indicator, in good time.

Centre:
You should look to your right in good time, for doing so will give you time to take appropriate action. A bus can be seen approaching a mini roundabout from the right.

Bottom:
Because of its length the bus turning left at the mini roundabout will have to use all the road available. Therefore, wait on the approach until the bus has completed its manoeuvre, otherwise a potentially dangerous situation may occur.

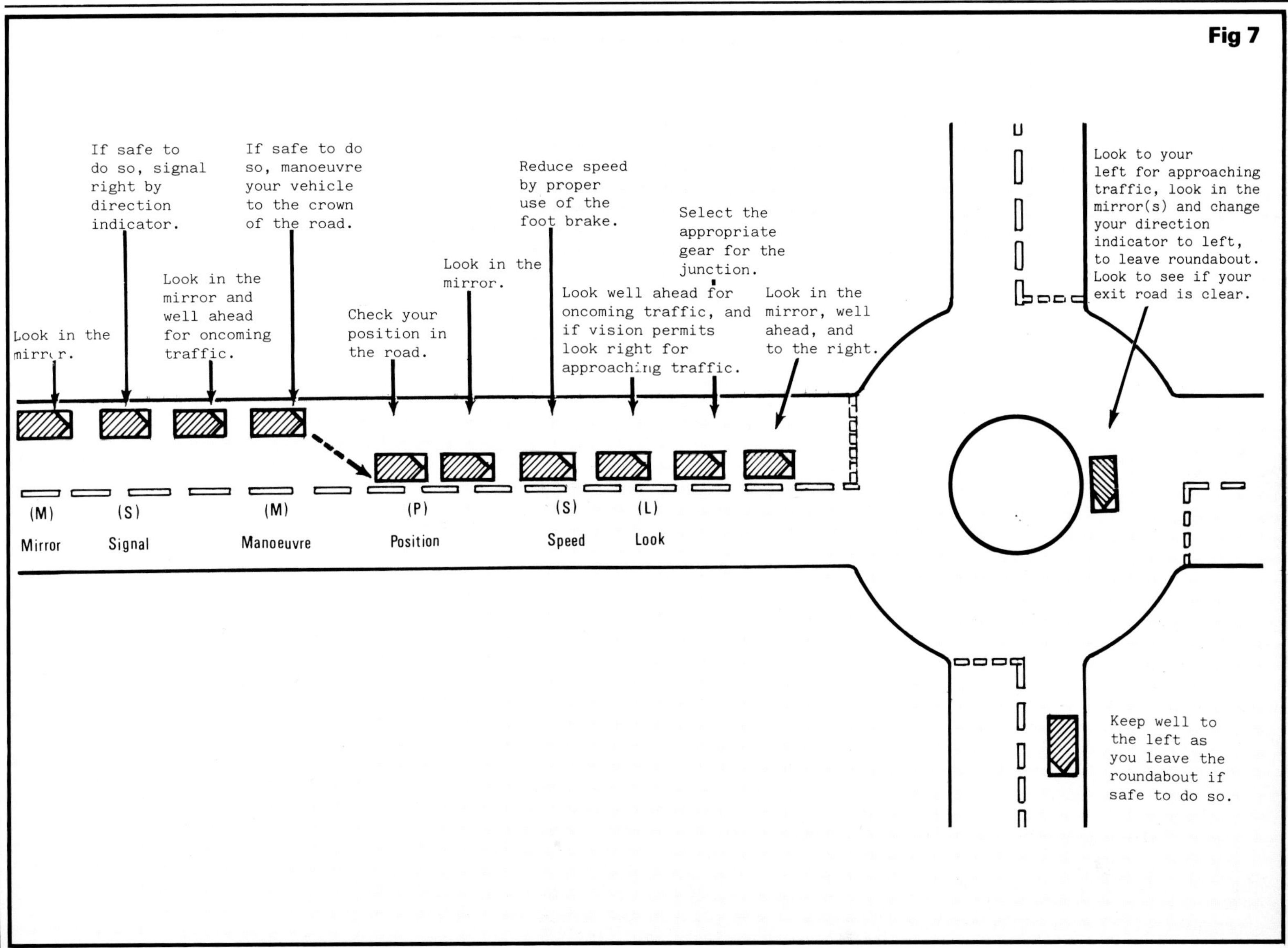

Turning right at a crossroads.

Top left:
Because of its size, go round a mini-roundabout at a speed at which you can steer your vehicle properly without swinging wide. Keep off the roundabout.

Bottom left:
Roundabouts vary in size and shape from the one-way 'mini' roundabout to the large gyratory complex, with two-way traffic on it. The general rule on any roundabout is to give way to traffic from the immediate right, unless road markings indicate otherwise.

Left:
If you do not look across the roundabout as you join it you could create a potentially dangerous situation. The group of people who have walked across the roundabout are about to cross the road.

Bottom left:
Look well ahead so that you can plan and position your vehicle in good time.

Turning right across a dual carriageway

As you approach a dual carriageway you must apply the system in good time so that you can assess the junction well before you reach it. If the central reserve is too narrow for the length of your vehicle you should wait at the junction until you can cross the dual carriageway in one movement. You must look right, left and right again as appropriate.

Below left:
Be extra careful when crossing or turning right into a dual carriageway. You should, if possible, position your vehicle in the correct lane for the direction you intend to go.

Below:
If the central reserve is wide enough for your vehicle, treat each half as a separate road, like this learner is doing.

Turning Right Faults

Turning Right Faults

Above:
The 'L' driver has turned too soon and has therefore cut a right-hand corner.

Right:
This driver has positioned the vehicle too late, therefore creating potential danger for other road users by blocking two lanes.

Position the vehicle correctly before turning left

A left turn can be just as dangerous as turning right if you do not carry out the system when and where practically possible. Consistent observation of movements of other traffic and pedestrians is vital.

In slow-moving traffic you must look over your left shoulder before you start to turn, otherwise you could collide with a cyclist or motorcyclist who may be coming up on your left. Also look out for extra long vehicles which are turning left and will be in a different position in the road to you for turning. Do not swing out before turning left. Look well ahead to give yourself time to position your vehicle correctly before and after turning left.

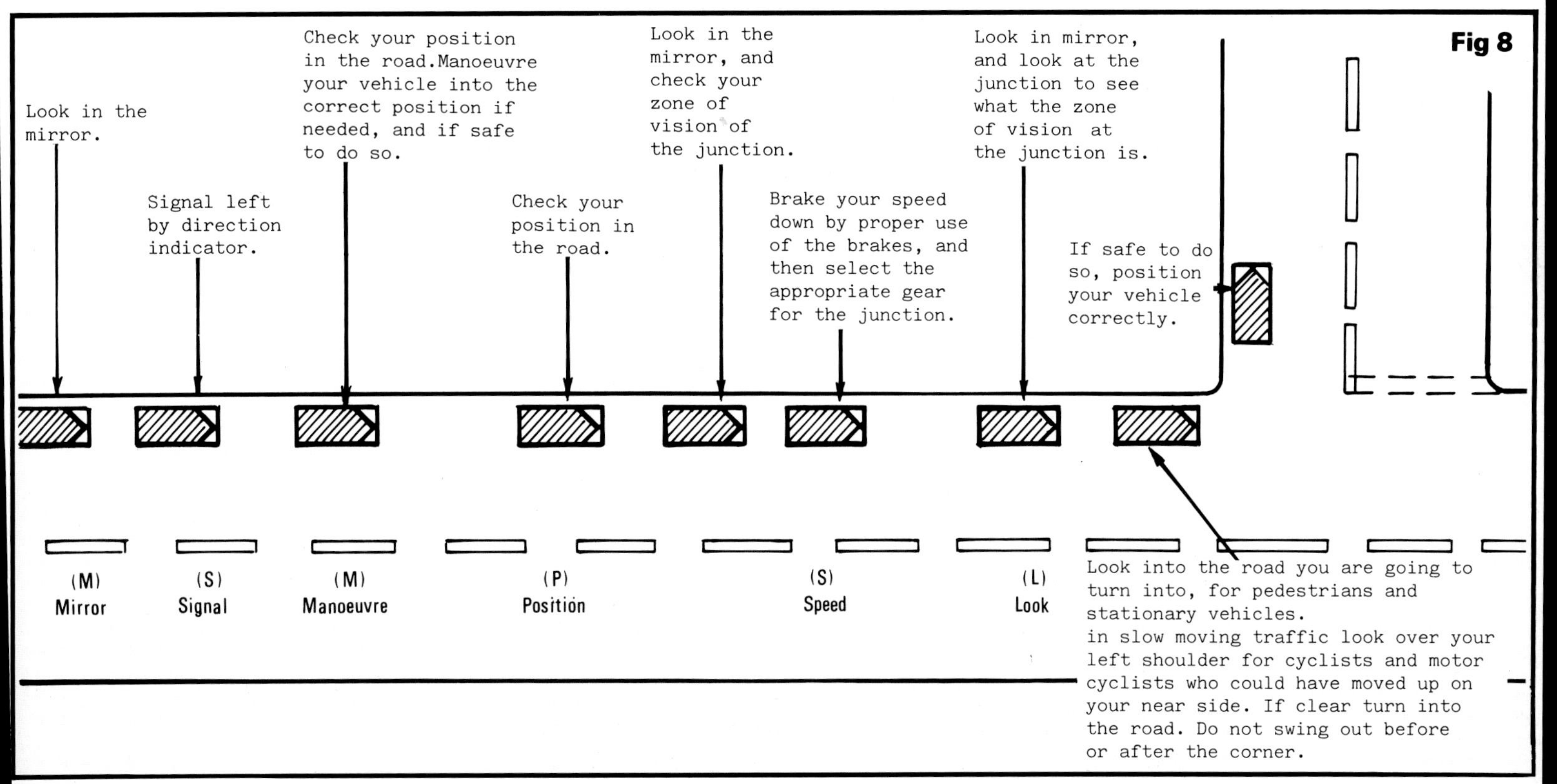

Turning left.

Top left:
This vehicle is in the correct position in the road for turning left. It is essential that you look into the road you are about to join before you leave your present position, otherwise you may have to pull up suddenly.

Bottom left:
If you position your vehicle as close to the kerb as this driver, your rear wheel could mount the kerb as it goes round the corner, creating danger to pedestrians who could be waiting to cross the road.

Top right:
This driver is inviting danger on his nearside, due to the incorrect position of his vehicle for turning left.

Bottom right:
This driver did not look well ahead and therefore has no driving plan. This is the reason why he is in the incorrect position for turning left; his path is obstructed by a stationary vehicle and at the same time is being overtaken.

Left:
If possible look into the road you are going to join so that you give yourself time to act on what you can see.

Summary

To follow the set sequence of movements outlined in good time before any hazard or junction.

Do not emerge at a junction until you are sure it is safe to do so; take into account any potential danger that could suddenly arise.

Think bike at junctions: you could miss them coming, it's harder for them to miss you.

Be extra careful if a commercial vehicle is approaching you when turning right and you have to pass nearside to nearside at a crossroad because your vision of oncoming traffic will be obscured by the large vehicle.

At roundabouts get in the correct lane for the direction you intend to go in good time as indicated by lane markings, direction signs or as mentioned in the *Highway Code*.

When turning right make a 90 degree turn when possible. Do not cut corners.

Look at the junction in good time to assess the zone of vision and any other hazards.

Anticipate the actions of heavy goods vehicles (which can be long vehicles) in good time as they need much more room to manoeuvre than a private car, especially at junctions and on roundabouts.

6 Driving

Overtaking

Overtake/meet/cross the path of/other vehicles safely

The key to successful overtaking — as with every driving manoeuvre — is careful observation. The observant driver will plan his driving well ahead so that full advantage of what can be seen on the road can be taken into account. He will assess the road he cannot see to be clear, taking into account possible changes in situation which could occur while making a manoeuvre. Only after taking these facts into consideration can a decision to overtake be made. Even then the driver must be able to stop his vehicle should the situation change rapidly: this is to make sure that he will not be involved with mistakes which could be made by other road users. When you have decided to overtake or make any manoeuvre, it is of the utmost importance that you look first in the mirror so that you can see what traffic, if any, is following, or indeed, overtaking you. If safe to do so indicate that you are going to move out to the right, then complete the manoeuvre in the shortest possible time, indicating when safely past the overtaken vehicle that you intend to move back into the normal driving position.

Right:
This learner has a clear road ahead but has not allowed enough distance before returning to the left and has 'cut-in'. The driver who is being overtaken is braking hard to avoid a collision. This is a dangerous fault.

Top left:
A typical example of bad, impatient driving which puts the moped rider in immediate danger. As stated in the *Highway Code* 'do not overtake on a corner or bend'.

Top right:
With a parked vehicle and with a vehicle approaching, this driver is holding back until the road ahead is clear and it is safe to pass the stationary vehicle. If in doubt, wait.

Left:
This driver has not allowed adequate room for safety while passing a stationary vehicle. This has created a potentially dangerous situation

Top left:
A typical example of dangerous overtaking which has a nickname — the meat sandwich. Should the driver of the blue car change course, the learner has left no room to manoeuvre, therefore creating a potentially dangerous situation.

Bottom left:
This driver has overtaken a young cyclist and then turned left across her path, creating a dangerous situation.

Top right:
If a test is taken in a rural area, extra caution must be taken when you meet or follow an agricultural vehicle. In this situation a tractor towing an agricultural trailer can be seen ahead. Ahead of the tractor an opening to the right can be seen: further along the road a left-hand bend can be seen and therefore it is not safe to overtake the tractor.

Bottom right:
Without any warning the tractor turns right. There are no direction indicator signals fitted to the tractor or trailer. The external rear view mirror has been folded back, rendering it useless; no arm signal was given, either. If in any doubt, always wait until you are sure it is safe to overtake.

Meet Other Vehicles Safely

Cross Their Path Safely

Meet Other Vehicles Safely

Far left:
This driver should have waited for the approaching vehicle to pass before moving out to pass the stationary vehicle. But he failed to do so and has therefore created a potentially dangerous situation.

Bottom left:
The learner thought he had the right of way. He didn't and consequently has created a potentially dangerous situation because he did not meet another vehicle safely. If an approaching vehicle flashes his headlights it is a warning of his presence and not an invitation for you to proceed.

Cross the Path of Other Vehicles Safely

Above right:
This driver has underestimated the speed and distance of the approaching vehicle and crossed its path forcing the other driver to brake hard to avoid a collision. A dangerous fault has been committed.

Position the vehicle correctly during normal driving

In normal driving conditions it is important that you keep well to the left when safe to do so. The exceptions to this are: when you intend to overtake another road user or turn right; if a bus lane is on your left; or if for any other reason a change in road position is needed. If you don't keep to the left you could baulk the path of other road users.

Avoid hugging the middle of the road or driving too close to the kerb as you could create a potentially dangerous situation for other road users and pedestrians.

A normal driving position in the road is when the nearside wheels of the vehicle are about one metre from the kerb. During normal driving, look well ahead to avoid having to make sudden movements of the steering wheel to change course.

Right:
With a clear road ahead this learner has positioned his vehicle in the correct position in the road for normal driving.

Top left:
This learner is driving too close to the kerb which could be potentially dangerous to other road users, pedestrians and the vehicle.

Bottom left:
No other road user can overtake the learner safely without being a potential danger to other road users, because the learner is driving too far from the left.

Top right:
If you approach a narrow bridge keep well to the left and anticipate approaching traffic not in view.

Bottom right:
Because of the ill-defined kerb-line at night, white lines have been painted on the road to assist users. The learner driver is on the wrong side of the lines where there is no need to do so, therefore encouraging another road user to overtake in a dangerous place.

Allow adequate clearance to stationary vehicles

When passing stationary vehicles, cyclists or pedestrians, you must allow adequate room in case a vehicle pulls out, or a door is opened. A pedestrian could step out between parked vehicles, cyclists may serve or wobble. If you do not allow adequate room when passing stationary vehicles you could create a potentially dangerous situation.

Top Left:
The area of road between the kerb and the continuous white line is for cyclists, therefore the correct position on the road is as shown.

Bottom left:
When a bus lane is present you must comply with the information given on the traffic sign. After 10am the bus lane can be used by all other road users.

Top right:
The learner has not allowed adequate clearance as he passed the stationary vehicle. Should the driver in the stationary car open his door, a potentially dangerous situation would occur.

Bottom right:
A rural high street has many seen and unseen dangers. Should you drive too close to the left, and a vehicle starts to reverse on to the main road as the vehicle in front is doing, a potentially dangerous situation could occur.

Take appropriate action at pedestrian crossings

Your speed on the approach to a Zebra or Pelican Crossing must be decided by the visibility or by the conditions prevailing, such as a slippery road surface, or the volume of pedestrian and/or vehicular traffic which obstructs your view of the crossing. You must approach a crossing at a proper speed so that you can pull up safely as and when necessary.

You *ought* to give way to pedestrians who are waiting on the edge of the pavement to use the crossing; you *must* give way to pedestrians who are on the crossing. Look out for blind people who may be carrying a white stick. A white stick with two red reflector bands on it indicates they are deaf as well so they will not hear your vehicle approaching.

On the approach to a Pelican Crossing, if the amber light is flashing you may go on, unless there are any pedestrians on the crossing in which case they have the right of way. When a pedestrian is on the crossing and you are the first on the approach, give the appropriate arm signal (I intend to slow down or stop), so that other road users and pedestrians are aware of your intentions.

Be extra careful when you approach a crossing in a busy shopping street. Commercial vehicles making their deliveries can restrict a driver's view of a crossing.

Top:
Should you be the first vehicle on the approach to a Zebra Crossing and a pedestrian is waiting to cross, you must give the appropriate arm signal to indicate your intention to slow down or stop as the situation demands. In doing so pedestrian(s) and other road users will be aware of your intentions. Note the 'I intend to slow down or stop' arm signal being given by the learner driver.

Bottom:
This driver has got the window closed and therefore will not be able to give the appropriate arm signal of his intention to slow down or stop, which is needed in this situation.

Top:
You must give way to pedestrians who are on the crossing — unlike this driver who has created a dangerous situation for the pedestrian.

Bottom:
Never invite pedestrians to cross the road like this driver is doing as a dangerous situation could occur.

Far right:
When you pull up make sure it is safe to do so. This 'L' driver has not done so and has blocked a private driveway thus causing inconvenience to another road user who is going to use the driveway.

Select a safe position for normal stops

Whenever the examiner requests you to pull up on the left at a convenient place, select a suitable place so that you do not create potential danger or inconvenience other road users or pedestrians. Should the examiner ask you to pull up at a particular place, do as requested. He will not try to catch you out in this, or any other situation during the test.

DEPT. OF TRANSPORT
APPROVED DRIVING INST.
VAUXHALL
CAVALIER SRi
F41 GNM
E760 AKJ

Right:
This driver is not complying with the road markings which are outside a school and this creates a potentially dangerous situation.

Tyre Care

Top:
Whenever the examiner requests you to pull up on the left, park the vehicle by the edge of the road. You should be able to do so without the tyres touching the kerb. Allow a gap (as shown) between the kerb and the wheels to avoid damage to the tyres. Pull up when the vehicle is parallel with the kerb.

Bottom:
When you park your vehicle by the edge of the road do not touch the kerb, otherwise you could cause excessive tyre damage which could be potentially dangerous to yourself, passengers and other road users.

Tyre Care

Show awareness and anticipation of the actions of pedestrians/cyclists/drivers

To be aware of, and able to anticipate, the actions of pedestrians, cyclists and drivers, the learner must always concentrate completely. If your mind wanders, the driving lesson or journey could end in disaster. Many people take driving a vehicle for granted. Regardless of what is on their mind at the time, they get into a vehicle and go through the motions of driving completely unaware of what is happening around them. Consequently they get involved in potentially dangerous situations which should have been recognised and acted on long before they occurred.

A good driver who is giving maximum concentration, coupled with good observation, will be able to anticipate potential danger and will therefore have time to act and formulate a safe driving plan, thus avoiding the danger.

Pedestrians

When driving along a busy street which has a lot of pedestrian traffic, if practically possible, allow adequate room for safety as you pass the pedestrians, especially young children whose movements are very unpredictable. If you pass pedestrians too closely you could create a dangerous situation.

When there are a lot of parked vehicles be extra careful as you pass them. Pedestrians do not always look where they are going and could walk out from behind them into your path.

Always drive at a speed so that you can pull up safely well within the distance you can see to be clear. Be aware of the movements of senior citizens who often — because of their failing eyesight — look while crossing the road instead of before.

Far left:
The information given by the traffic sign is self-explanatory, but the warning given is often ignored by many road users. Be prepared to meet pedestrians, especially on the approach to a left-hand bend, and adjust your speed accordingly.

Top right:
Whenever you approach stationary vehicles, look ahead and if possible underneath them. Can you seen the potential danger?

Bottom right:
If you did not see the potential danger, this is what you could see as the children emerge from behind the parked vehicle. Look well ahead and plan your driving, otherwise a potentially dangerous situation could occur.

Below:
This pedestrian is crossing the road, but has not checked to make sure it was safe to do so and is therefore unaware of approaching traffic. If a driver has not anticipated this, a potentially dangerous situation will occur.

Right:
Make allowances for pedestrians with poor eyesight or who are elderly. They might not see you, or underestimate your speed or distance from them.

Bottom right:
This driver has not allowed adequate clearance for safety while passing the cyclist who could, for one reason or another, swerve or wobble, which could create a dangerous situation due to the lack of anticipation by the driver.

Cyclists

Like motorcyclists, cyclists are open to the elements, but are lighter than a motorcycle or moped and will therefore be affected by cross-winds, particularly in open roads or near tall buildings. When overtaking a cyclist allow plenty of room in case they wobble or swerve, especially when the weather is windy or it is raining. A cyclist is open to all elements of danger — you are not.

In slow-moving traffic a cyclist may move up on your left. Always remember to make sure it is safe to turn left at a junction, by looking over your left shoulder.

Look out for cyclists who leave a cycle track or other junction without looking. If you intend to cross a cycle track look out for cyclists and moped riders who could be going faster than you think. Not all the cyclists who use our overcrowded roads have been trained to the National Cycling Proficiency Standard, therefore allow for the mistakes which the untrained rider may make.

Above left:
The cyclist should have given way to the 'L' driver. The 'L' driver should have anticipated the cyclists action, he did not therefore a potential situation has occurred.

Left:
This driver did not anticipate the cyclist moving off or allow adequate clearance when passing stationary vehicles, which has added danger to the situation.

Drivers

A good driver who is concentrating all the time, combined with effective observation, will recognise potential danger in good time. He will anticipate the actions of other drivers and motorcyclists, taking nothing for granted. An alert driver never gets caught unaware or gets involved with other road users' mistakes.

Top left:
The approaching vehicle is signalling to turn left. Never assume a vehicle will turn. Wait until you see some other positive action, ie reduction of speed or vehicle beginning to turn before emerging.

Bottom left:
This 'L' driver has followed another vehicle too closely. Because the 'L' driver did not anticipate the vehicle in front stopping, he has got himself boxed in.

Top right:
The bus driver has signalled his intention to move out. If practically possible and safe to do so without creating potential danger to other road users, give way to the bus.

Bottom right:
Where there are a lot of parked vehicles, keep a safe distance from them as you pass. This driver did not and therefore has not been seen by the driver who is reversing. Always try to anticipate the actions of others, and in good time.

Far right:
The 'L' driver is following too closely to the vehicle in front and therefore has not got time to anticipate the actions of the other driver. Leave enough space between you and the vehicles in front. Remember the two-second rule and apply it.

DEPT. OF TRANSPORT
APPROVED DRIVING INST.
F41 GNM

Drivers and the two-second rule

What is the two-second rule? It is a method of keeping a safe distance between you and the vehicle in front, at any speed. When the road surface is wet and in adverse weather conditions the distance between you and the vehicle in front should be doubled and on motorways trebled.

On the open road, 1yd for every one mile per hour should be maintained — so a car travelling on a dry road at 50mph should have a gap of 50yd from the vehicle in front. As the speed increases so does the distance from the vehicle in front. As a guide, when driving in built up areas at a speed below 10mph a minimum distance of 1ft for every one mile per hour should be allowed. As you leave the built-up area and your speed increases, so should the distance from the vehicle in front increase. It doesn't take much to have an accident if you're following too closely: the road surface, poor brakes, worn tyres, an instant's loss of concentration, no brake lights on the vehicle in front — any of these could lead to a collision. There are many drivers today who wish they had kept a safe distance from the vehicle in front of them.

ONLY A FOOL BREAKS THE TWO-SECOND RULE.

Above:
When turning into another road allow a safe distance from the vehicle in front. This driver is following the moped rider too closely and is creating a potentially dangerous situation.

Right:
You must leave enough space between you and the vehicle in front so that you can pull up safely. The distance between the two vehicles in this picture is approximately 23m at 30mph and is known as the 'separation distance'. Under ideal conditions, 23m is the shortest stopping distance. On a wet road surface, separation and stopping distance must be doubled.

Fig 9

Drivers and the two-second rule.

Left:
The distance between these two vehicles is approximately 53m, this being the shortest stopping distance on a dry road at 50mph. On a wet road surface, separation and stopping distance must be doubled.

Summary

Do not overtake unless you can complete the manoeuvre safely.

Meet other vehicles safely by letting the oncoming vehicle have the right of way.

Do not cross the path of other vehicles. Estimate the speed and distance of oncoming vehicles and wait until the oncoming traffic has passed if you cannot complete your turn safely.

Drive in the correct position in the road when safe to do so.

Whatever you pass as you drive along, allow adequate clearance for safety.

At pedestrian crossings, give way to pedestrians who are waiting to cross the road.

Pull up at safe places when requested to do so by the examiner.

Look well ahead — then you will be able to anticipate the actions of other road users, without being taken by surprise. This will mean hurried movements and impaired control, which could create a potentially dangerous situation.

7 The End of the Test

The *Highway Code*

At the end of the test drive the examiner will ask you to pull up. You will be approximately where you first started. When your vehicle has stopped, apply the handbrake and move the gear lever into neutral. The examiner will ask you to stop your engine.

The examiner will now say 'Now I should like to put a few questions on the *Highway Code* and other motoring matters'. Remember that this is still part of the driving test. He will take out of his document wallet a book with a picture of a traffic sign on each page. The examiner will turn the pages over and ask you what the signs mean. You will be asked to identify about six signs and then he will ask you questions on the *Highway Code* and other motoring matters. Some typical questions are:

'How would you join a motorway safely?'

'What are the main causes of skidding?'

'How would you drive in fog?'

'What would you do if you were dazzled by headlights at night?'

'What is the overall stopping distance at 60mph?'

'What is the first thing you would do if involved in an accident?'

After the questions the examiner will say, 'That's the end of the test — I'm pleased to tell you that you've passed', or 'That's the end of the test — I'm sorry you haven't passed but your driving hasn't reached the required standard'. It's the last comment we don't want to hear, do we?

It is of the utmost importance that you study the *Highway Code* and that you know the contents when you go for your test.

Statistics on the reasons for test failures are included to give you further insight into the test.

Conclusion of the Test

Pass

The examiner will say 'That's the end of the test and I'm pleased to tell you that you've passed. Is your address still the same as the one on your application form? May I see your driving licence, please. Will you sign this pass certificate, please. Make sure you send this certificate when you next apply for a driving licence. Thank you, good day'.

Fail

The examiner will say, 'That's the end of the test — I'm sorry you haven't passed, but your driving hasn't reached the required standard. If you'll give me a few moments I'll help you by marking the points to which you should give special attention. Good day'.

To assist you with your highway code questions a book titled *Drive and Survive* published by Kogan Page will be of assistance to you. It is a multi-choice answer book. Also to help you understand and learn road craft more quickly a book titled *Advanced Driving* by Gordon Cole is published by Ian Allan Ltd. Both books are available from all good bookshops.